Michael Miller

Sams **Teach Yourself**

YouTube™

in **10 Minutes**

 800 East 96th Street, Indianapolis, Indiana 46240

Sams Teach Yourself YouTube™ in 10 Minutes

ISBN-13: 978-0-672-33086-5
ISBN-10: 0-672-33086-5

Library of Congress Cataloging-in-Publication Data
Miller, Michael, 1958-
Sams teach yourself YouTube in 10 minutes / Michael Miller.
    p. cm.
Includes index.
ISBN 978-0-672-33086-5
1. YouTube (Electronic resource) 2. Internet videos. 3. Online social networks. 4. YouTube (Firm) I. Title. II. Title: YouTube in 10 minutes.
TK5105.8868.Y68M665 2009
006.7–dc22

2009027627

Printed in the United States of America

First Printing August 2009

Trademarks

All terms mentioned in this book that are known to be trademarks or service marks have been appropriately capitalized. Sams Publishing cannot attest to the accuracy of this information. Use of a term in this book should not be regarded as affecting the validity of any trademark or service mark.

Warning and Disclaimer

Every effort has been made to make this book as complete and as accurate as possible, but no warranty or fitness is implied. The information provided is on an "as is" basis. The author and the publisher shall have neither liability nor responsibility to any person or entity with respect to any loss or damages arising from the information contained in this book.

Bulk Sales

Sams Publishing offers excellent discounts on this book when ordered in quantity for bulk purchases or special sales. For more information, please contact

U.S. Corporate and Government Sales

1-800-382-3419

corpsales@pearsontechgroup.com

For sales outside of the U.S., please contact

International Sales

international@pearson.com

Associate Publisher
Greg Wiegand

Acquisitions Editor
Michelle Newcomb

Development Editor
Wordsmithery LLC

Managing Editor
Patrick Kanouse

Project Editor
Mandie Frank

Copy Editor
BoxTwelve

Indexer
Erika Millen

Proofreader
Kathy Ruiz

Technical Editor
Vince Averello

Publishing Coordinator
Cindy Teeters

Designer
Gary Adair

Compositor
Bronkella Publishing LLC

Contents

About the Author

Michael Miller has written more than 90 non-fiction books over the past two decades. His best-selling titles include *YouTube 4 You, YouTube for Business, Absolute Beginner's Guide to Computer Basics, Googlepedia: The Ultimate Google Resource*, and *Speed It Up! A Non-Technical Guide for Speeding Up Slow Computers.* He has established a reputation for practical advice, technical accuracy, and an unerring empathy for the needs of his readers. For more information about Mr. Miller and his writing, visit his website at www.molehillgroup.com or email him at youtube10@molehillgroup.com.

Dedication

To Sherry: Ten minutes isn't long enough.

Acknowledgments

Special thanks to the usual suspects at Que, including but not limited to Greg Wiegand, Michelle Newcomb, Charlotte Kughen, Mandie Frank, Jeff Riley, and technical editor Vince Averello.

We Want to Hear from You!

As the reader of this book, *you* are our most important critic and commentator. We value your opinion and want to know what we're doing right, what we could do better, what areas you'd like to see us publish in, and any other words of wisdom you're willing to pass our way.

You can email or write me directly to let me know what you did or didn't like about this book—as well as what we can do to make our books stronger.

Please note that I cannot help you with technical problems related to the topic of this book, and that due to the high volume of mail I receive, I might not be able to reply to every message.

When you write, please be sure to include this book's title and author as well as your name and phone or email address. I will carefully review your comments and share them with the author and editors who worked on the book.

E-mail: consumer@samspublishing.com

Mail: Greg Wiegand
       Associate Publisher
       Sams Publishing
       800 East 96th Street
       Indianapolis, IN 46240 USA

Reader Services

Visit our website and register this book at www.informit.com/title/9780672330865 for convenient access to any updates, downloads, or errata that might be available for this book.

Introduction

YouTube is full of videos, millions of them. Entertaining videos. Informative videos. Instructional videos. You name it, somebody has probably uploaded a video about it.

But how do you find the videos you want to watch? And how do you share the videos you find? And what about uploading your own videos— and managing the videos you upload? Just how do you figure out this whole YouTube thing, without spending hours and hours of your precious time?

Well, that's where this book comes in. *Sams Teach Yourself YouTube in 10 Minutes* is a quick and easy way to learn how to view and upload YouTube videos. Every lesson in this book is short and to the point, so you can learn everything you need to learn at your own pace, in your own time. Just follow the straightforward *Sams Teach Yourself in 10 Minutes* game plan: short, goal-oriented lessons that can make you productive with each topic in 10 minutes or less.

What You Need to Know Before You Use This Book

How much prior experience do you need before starting this book? Absolutely none! You don't have to be an active viewer or an experienced video producer. All you need is a computer with an Internet connection. Everything you need to know flows from there.

About the *Sams Teach Yourself in 10 Minutes* Series

Sams Teach Yourself YouTube in 10 Minutes uses a series of short lessons that walk you through the various aspect of the YouTube site. Each lesson is designed to take about 10 minutes and each is limited to a particular operation or group of features. Most of the instruction is presented in easy-to-follow numbered steps, and there are plenty of examples and screen shots to show you what things look like along the way. By the time you finish this book, you should feel confident in using the YouTube site to both view and upload all sorts of videos.

Special Sidebars

In addition to the normal text and figures, you'll find what we call *sidebars* scattered throughout that highlight special kinds of information. These are intended to help you save time and to teach you important information fast.

> **PLAIN ENGLISH**
>
> Plain English sidebars call your attention to definitions of new terms. If you aren't familiar with some of the terms and concepts, watch for these flagged paragraphs.

> **CAUTION**
>
> Cautions alert you to common mistakes and tell you how to avoid them.

> **TIP**
>
> Tips explain inside hints for using YouTube more efficiently.

> **NOTE**
>
> Notes present pertinent pieces of information related to the surrounding discussion.

Getting to Know YouTube

In this lesson, you learn how to find your way around the YouTube website—and create a YouTube account.

Welcome to YouTube

YouTube is a video sharing community. That means that YouTube users can both upload and view all sorts of video clips online, using any web browser.

As the largest video sharing community on the web, YouTube has become a repository for literally millions of movie clips, TV clips (both current and classic), music videos, and home videos. The most popular YouTube videos quickly become "viral," getting passed around from person to person via email and linked to from other sites and from other blogs on the web. If a YouTube video is particularly interesting, you'll see it pop up virtually everywhere, from TV's *The Daily Show* to the front page of your favorite website.

Part of YouTube's appeal is its ease of use. Finding a video is as easy as performing a keyword search; watching a video requires nothing more than the click of a Play button; and uploading a video is also pretty much a one-button operation. The YouTube site itself does all the heavy lifting in terms of technology, including file conversion, hosting, and serving. YouTube even lets you send video links to your friends and family via email, and you can host those links on your own website or blog.

So whether you like to watch or like to share, YouTube gives you what you want, the way you want it. That's why it's been so successful.

What's Playing On YouTube

What can you find on the YouTube site? It's safe to say that just about any kind of video you're interested in, YouTube has it—or something like it.

Most of the videos on YouTube come from individuals, just like you and me. Many of these videos are simple home movies, of everything from birthday parties to school plays. Others are so-called *video blogs* (dubbed *vlogs*), where users talk about anything and everything that's on their minds. Anybody with a video camera can easily upload their home movies to YouTube and make them available for the whole world to see.

Other videos on YouTube are decidedly more professional. Budding film professionals can post their work on YouTube, which essentially converts the site into a giant repository of filmmakers' resumés. Student films, spec videos, acting and directing tryouts—they're all there.

YouTube is also a repository for "historical" items. We're talking old television commercials, music videos, clips from classic television shows, you name it. Want to revisit your childhood and watch an old Maypo commercial? There are several on YouTube. How about a clip of the Ronettes performing on the old *Shindig!* show? Or the Beatles on the *Ed Sullivan Show*? Or the opening credits to the old *Astro Boy* cartoon? They're all there, believe it or not. YouTube is a great site for nostalgia buffs, collectors, and the like.

Speaking of music videos, there is no better site on the web to find your favorite video clips. YouTube offers music videos from all manner of artists, in every conceivable genre. For record labels, YouTube is a great place to promote hot new music and bands. If you're a music lover, you'll love YouTube.

There's even a lot of television shows and movies on YouTube. The site's Shows categories features television programming from ABC, CBS, PBS, the BBC, Discovery Channel, National Geographic, TLC, Showtime, Starz, and more; the Movies category features current and classic movies. And it's all free.

So what's on YouTube tonight? As you can see, a little bit of everything!

How YouTube Works

It may seem simple to watch a video (just click the play button), but when you view a video on YouTube there's a lot of technology involved behind the scenes.

It all starts with the uploading of video files. Users upload videos to YouTube in QuickTime, AVI, MPEG, or Windows Media Video (WMV) file formats. YouTube then converts these video files into Flash format—which is how the videos are served to YouTube users. (To view YouTube videos in your web browser, you must have Macromedia Flash Player 7 installed.) All the videos are stored on YouTube's servers and served via streaming video to viewers' web browsers.

Since YouTube utilizes streaming video technology, video files are not saved to your hard disk. That's because streaming video is different from downloading a complete video file. When you download a file, you can't start playing that file until it is completely downloaded to your PC. With streaming video, however, playback can start before an entire file is downloaded; the first part of the file is present on your PC while the last part is still downloading. It makes for almost-immediate video playback, especially if you have a broadband Internet connection—which means immediate gratification for YouTube viewers!

> PLAIN ENGLISH: **Streaming Video**
> Technology that enables immediate playback of video files without first downloading those files to a computer.

Navigating YouTube's Home Page

When you first access YouTube (www.youtube.com), you see the home page shown in Figure 1.1. This is your home base for the entire site; from here you can browse videos, search for videos, access your favorite videos, and even upload your own videos.

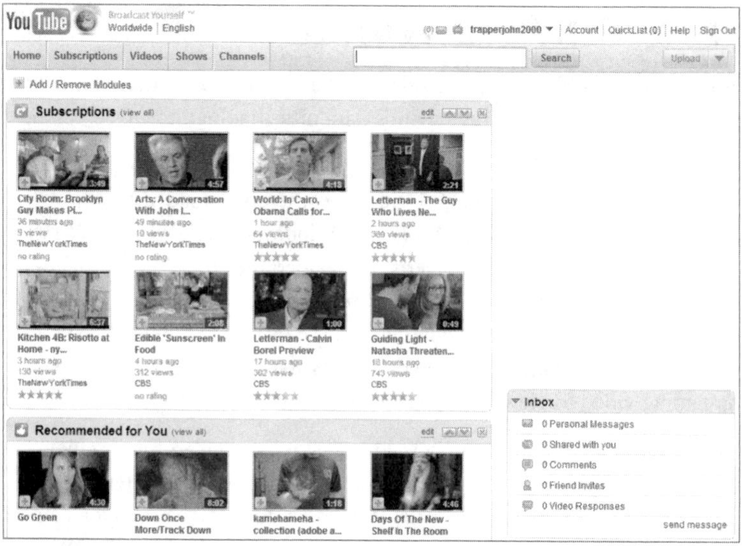

FIGURE 1.1   The YouTube home page.

> NOTE: **YouTube Accounts**
>
> YouTube's home page looks slightly different if you haven't yet sub-
> scribed or signed in. You need to create a (free) YouTube account
> and sign in to get access to all of the site's features. Learn more in
> the "Creating a YouTube Account" section, later in this lesson.

There are a lot of items on this home page, including the following:

▶ At the very top of the page, links to your YouTube email inbox,
  videos you're sharing, your YouTube account, a QuickList of
  videos you've tagged for future viewing, and YouTube's help
  system.

▶ Also at the top of the page (when you click your account name),
  links to videos you've uploaded (My Videos), along with links to
  your favorite videos, playlists, videos you've subscribed to, your
  email inbox, and more.

▶ A toolbar that includes a search box, Upload button (for uploading your own videos) and buttons that link to important parts of the YouTube site—the Home page, your Subscriptions, Videos by category, commercial TV Shows for viewing, and Channels for all YouTube users.

▶ An Inbox box that displays messages, comments, friend invites, and the like.

▶ A What's New box that tells you all about YouTube's latest features.

▶ Spotlight—videos that YouTube is highlighting at the moment.

▶ Subscriptions—videos from users to whom you've subscribed.

▶ Recommended for You—videos that YouTube thinks you might like, based on your past viewing.

▶ Friends—the most recent videos from your YouTube friends.

▶ Featured Videos—the hottest or coolest videos on YouTube today.

▶ Videos Being Watched Now—what other viewers are watching at this moment.

▶ Finally, at the very bottom of the home page, you'll find links to other essential site features—including help and company information.

To move to a different part of the YouTube site, just click the appropriate button or link. For example, to manage your account information, click the Account link at the top of the page. To browse through videos by category, click the Videos button. Or to view the videos you yourself have uploaded, click the right arrow next to your user name at the top of the page, then click My Videos.

To view a video displayed on YouTube's home page, just click the thumbnail for that video. That will open that video's viewing page and start playback of the video.

Customizing the Home Page

One of the neat things about YouTube is how easy it is to customize it to your own personal taste. For the home page, this means adding and removing specific content modules.

To change the content of YouTube's home page, follow these steps:

1. Click the Add/Remove Modules link, shown in Figure 1.2.

FIGURE 1.2   Click to customize YouTube's home page.

2. When the Customize Home Page appears, as shown in Figure 1.3, check those modules you want to display and uncheck those you don't want to see.

3. Click the Save Changes button.

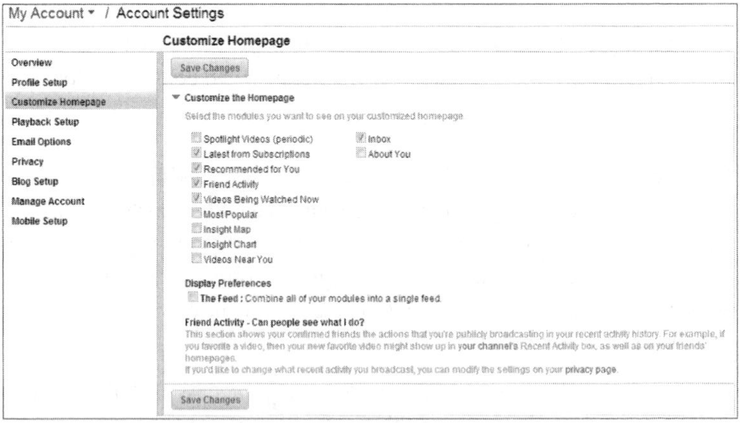

FIGURE 1.3   Customizing YouTube's home page.

Getting Help

If you can't quite figure out what's where or just need help completing a specific operation, click the Help link at the top of YouTube's home page. This opens YouTube Help page, shown in Figure 1.4. Click the General Help Center link to browse through articles that guide you through various aspects of the YouTube experience, or use the Search box to search through all available Help Center topics.

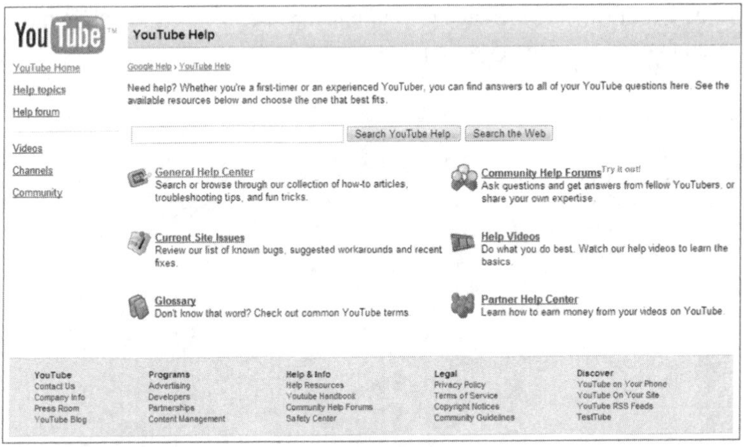

FIGURE 1.4 The YouTube Help page.

Creating a YouTube Account

To take full advantage of all of YouTube's features, you need to set up your own personal YouTube account. Naturally, you need an account before you can upload any videos to the site. But you also need an account to save your favorite videos, create playlists, join groups and communities, and the like.

> NOTE: **YouTube and Google**
> YouTube is owned by Google. As such, if you have a Google account, you can use that account to log onto the YouTube site.

Fortunately, it's both easy and free to create a YouTube account. Just go to
the home page and click the Sign Up link at the very top of the page.
YouTube now displays the Get Started with Your Account page, shown in
Figure 1.5. You'll need to choose a username, enter some personal information (your location, postal code, date of birth, and gender), and accept
YouTube's terms of use. Click the I Accept button and YouTube now asks
you to either add YouTube to your existing Google account (if you have
one) or create a new Google/YouTube account. If you already have a
Google account, you're done. If not, create a new account and YouTube
sends a confirmation message to your email address; click the link in this
email to confirm your subscription.

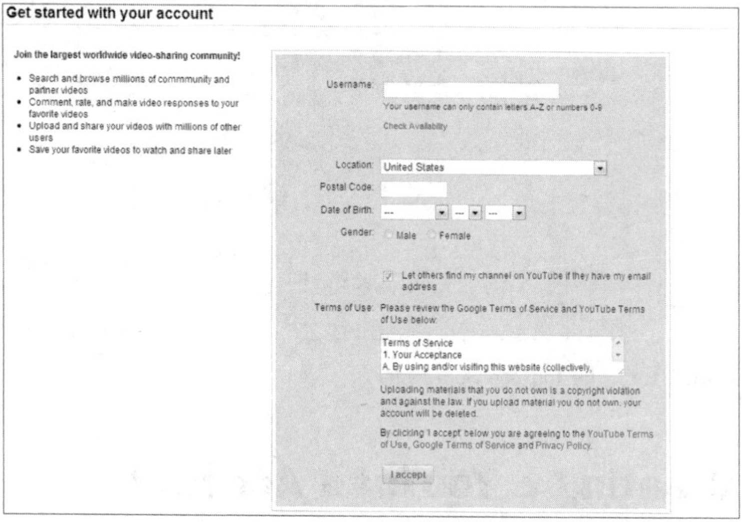

FIGURE 1.5   Signing up for a YouTube account.

Once you've created your account, you need to log into YouTube to use
the account. Do this by clicking the Sign In link at the top of the YouTube
home page; enter your user name and password, and you're ready to start
viewing!

Summary

In this lesson, you learned how to sign up for YouTube, navigate the home page, and find help. In the next lesson, you learn to search for videos on YouTube.

Browsing and Searching for Videos

In this lesson, you learn how to find videos to view on YouTube.

Browsing for Videos

As you learned in Lesson 1, "Getting to Know YouTube," there are two ways to find videos on YouTube—by browsing or by searching. Browsing is the way a lot of new users start out; it's a great way to discover new videos, just by clicking through the categories until you find something you like.

> CAUTION: **Limited Selection**
>
> The only problem with browsing is that you don't get to see everything that's available. Browsing by category exposes you only to a list of featured videos in that category, as selected by the YouTube staff—not to all videos available on the site.

Browsing by Category

For most users, the best way to browse YouTube is by category. To browse by category, follow these steps:

1. From any YouTube page, click the Videos button on the YouTube toolbar.

2. Click the category name in the Categories list on the left side of the page.

3. When the next page appears, as shown in Figure 2.1, click the Popular tab to view popular YouTube videos in that category, or the Most Viewed tab to view the most viewed videos in that category.

4. To view a specific video, click the thumbnail for that video.

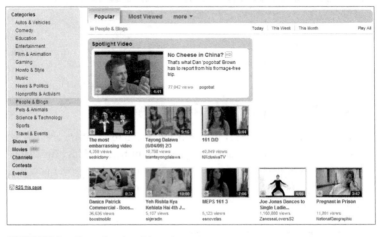

FIGURE 2.1   Browsing for videos by category.

> TIP: **More Options**
> Click the More link to view Spotlight Videos, Rising Videos, Most Discussed videos, Recent Videos, Most Responded to videos, Top Favorite videos, and Top Rated videos.

YouTube organizes its videos into the following major categories:

▶ **Autos & Vehicles**, the place for videos about planes, trains, and automobiles—car chases, monster truck rallies, flight films, you name it.

▶ **Comedy**, home of the funniest stuff on YouTube—from amateur video hijinks to standup comedy routines to clips from movie comedies.

► **Education**, with videos for, about, and from the education universe.

► **Entertainment**, which is kind of a hodgepodge of short movies, odd stuff, and other random entertainment.

► **Film & Animation**, which is where you find short art films, classic cartoons, animated shorts, computer-generation animation, and the like.

► **Gaming**, YouTube's collection of video game and PC game demos, previews, and examples of real-world game play.

► **Howto & Style**, where you can find step-by-step instructions to do just about anything you need to do—especially style-related topics.

► **Music**, one of YouTube's biggest categories, full of music videos and classic performance clips from major artists—as well as performances from amateur and up-and-coming musicians and user-compiled music montages.

► **News & Politics**, which is where you'll find the most newsworthy clips on the YouTube site—stories from professional journalists, live events captured by amateur video cameras, and more.

► **Nonprofits & Activism**, with videos for, about, and from the nonprofit community.

► **People & Blog**, which includes user-produced videos of all shapes and sizes, including personal video blogs.

► **Pets & Animals**, the place to find both Stupid Pet Tricks and cute animal videos.

► **Science & Technology**, which features videos about technology—computer how-tos, dancing robots, and various science-related clips.

► **Sports**, a vast repository of both professional and amateur sports highlights.

▶ **Travel & Events**, the place to find homemade travel videos and neat nature clips.

TIP: **Most Recent Videos**

Within any category, you can view the newest videos by clicking one of the links above the video list—Today, This Week, This Month, or All Time.

Browsing by Channel

Browsing by category isn't the only way to browse YouTube. YouTube also organizes videos by *channel*, which is a great way to find videos by people whose tastes you share.

PLAIN ENGLISH: **Channel**

A channel is a collection of all videos uploaded by a specific YouTube user; every YouTube user has his or her own channel.

To browse YouTube's featured channels, follow these steps:

1. From any YouTube page, click the Channels button on the YouTube toolbar.

2. Click a channel category from the Channels Categories list on the left side of the page.

3. When the next page appears, click the Most Subscribed tab to view the most subscribed-to channels on YouTube, or click the Most Viewed tab to view the most viewed channels.

4. To view the channel page for a specific user, click the username above a video thumbnail.

When you click a channel link, you see that user's channel page (see Figure 2.2). Channel pages display all the videos uploaded by that user, as well as that user's favorite videos, playlists, and other information.

FIGURE 2.2 A typical user channel page.

Browsing for TV Shows and Movies

YouTube not only includes videos uploaded by normal users, but also commercial TV shows and movies. To browse for this commercial content, follow these steps:

1. From any YouTube page, click the Shows button on the YouTube toolbar.

2. To browse for TV shows by category, click a category from the Shows list on the left side of the page, as shown in Figure 2.3.

3. To browse for movies by category, click the Movies link on the left side of the page, then click a category.

4. Click the Alphabetical tab to view shows and movies in alphabetical order; click the Most Recent tab to view the newest videos; click the Most Popular tab to view the most popular shows and movies; or click the Network tab to view all shows on a given network or to view movies produced by a given studio.

5. To view a TV show or movie, click the program's thumbnail image.

FIGURE 2.3   Viewing TV shows on YouTube.

All movies and TV shows on the YouTube site are free; you don't have to pay to view anything.

Searching YouTube

When you're not sure what you want to watch, browsing by category is probably the way to go. If you have a particular type of video in mind, however, searching is a better approach.

Conducting a Search

Searching YouTube is a simple process. At the top of every YouTube page is a search box. (Most pages also have a similar search box on the bottom of the page.) To search for a video, simply enter into this search box a keyword or two that describes what you're searching for, and then click the Search button.

For example, if you want to search for Coldplay videos, enter **coldplay** in the search box. (Capitalization isn't necessary.) To search for clips of dancing monkeys, enter **dancing monkeys**. And so forth.

Working with Search Results

When you click the Search button, YouTube returns a list of videos that best matches your search criteria, like the one shown in Figure 2.4. If you see a video you want to watch, just click it. Otherwise, you can narrow down a large list by using the links above the search results:

▶ **All, Channels, Playlists** filters your search to display all videos and related channels, channels only, or playlists only

▶ **Sort By** sorts your results by Relevance (default), Newest, Oldest, View Count, or Rating.

▶ **Uploaded** filters your results by when the videos were uploaded: Anytime (default), Today, This Week, or This Month.

▶ **Type** filters your results by type of video: All (default), Partner Videos, videos with Annotations, videos with Closed Captions, or HD videos.

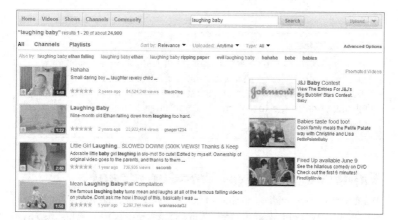

FIGURE 2.4 The results of a YouTube search.

CAUTION: **Promoted Videos**

Beware the so-called promoted videos along the side of most searched results pages. These are actually paid advertisements for those videos, not legitimate search results. (Learn more about promoted videos in Lesson 26, "Promoting Your YouTube Videos.")

Each search result contains the following information:

- ▶ Key frame from the video

- ▶ Title of the video

- ▶ Short description of the video

- ▶ Total length of the video, in minutes and seconds

- ▶ Star rating of the video (the rating is from 1 to 5 stars—more is better)

- ▶ When the video was added to YouTube

- ▶ Number of times the video has been viewed

- ▶ The user who uploaded the video (click the user's name to see all videos in his or her channel)

TIP: **QuickList**

See a video you'd like to watch, but don't want to watch right now? Then click the "+" sign at the bottom left of the video thumbnail; this adds the video to your QuickList. You can then click the QuickList link at the top of any YouTube page to revisit these flagged videos.

Exploring with the Wonder Wheel

Want to find more videos similar to the one you searched for? Then click the Wonder Wheel link at the top of any search results page. This displays a "wheel" of related search queries, like the one shown in Figure 2.5. Click any of the related queries to display even more queries related to that query (in a new spoke), as well as videos that match the selected query. It's a fun way to explore everything that YouTube has to offer!

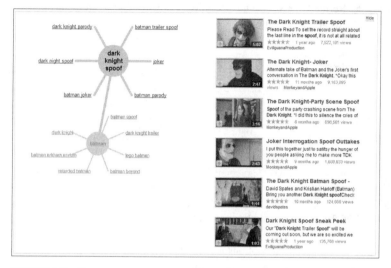

FIGURE 2.5 Expanding your search with the Wonder Wheel.

Advanced Searching

YouTube, like its parent Google, provides some advanced search options to help you further refine your search. You access these search options by clicking the Advanced Options link on any search results page.

The Advanced Search pane, shown in Figure 2.6, includes the following options:

- Filter Videos That May Not Be Suitable for Minors

- Find Results That Have All These Words, This Exact Phrase, One or More of These Words, or None of These Words

- Show These Types of Results: All, Videos, Channels, Playlists, Shows, or Movies

► Show Only Videos With These Features: HD (High Definition), Annotations, Closed Captions, or Promoted Videos

► Refine Your Search by: Duration, Category, Language, Uploaded (when), or Location

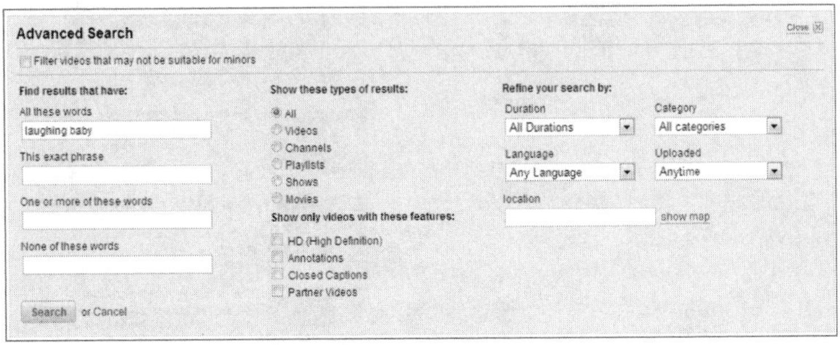

FIGURE 2.6   YouTube's advanced search options.

Check the appropriate options and enter the necessary keywords, then click the Search button to conduct the search.

> TIP: **Content Filter**
>
> To shield younger viewers from potentially offensive videos, check the Filter Videos That May Not Be Suitable for Minors option in the Advanced Search pane.

Summary

In this lesson, you learned how to find videos by both browsing and searching. In the next lesson, you learn how to watch the videos you find.

Watching a YouTube Video

In this lesson, you learn how to view videos on YouTube.

Navigating the Video Page

Once you've browsed to or searched for a video, you want to view that video. You do this by clicking the thumbnail for that video.

This displays a page for that video, like the one shown in Figure 3.1. There are several sections to this page, including:

1. **Video player**—where you watch the videos

2. **Information**—key facts about the video

3. **Related videos**—a great way to explore similar videos

4. **More from**—additional videos from this user

5. **Options**—for sharing and remembering this video

6. **Statistics & Data**—shows how popular this video is

7. **Comments and responses**—what other users think about this video

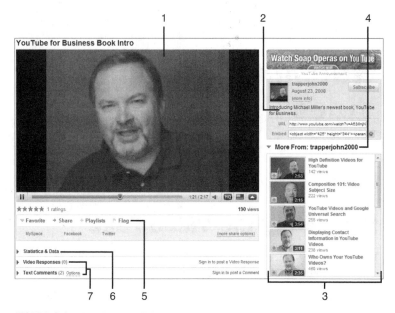

FIGURE 3.1   A typical YouTube video page.

Using the Video Player

The most important part of the video page is the video player; this is where the video plays back. In fact, playback is automatic—the video starts playing almost immediately after you click any video thumbnail to open the video's page.

> TIP: **Slow Connections**
>
> If you have a slow or congested Internet connection, some videos may pause or stutter periodically after playback has started. This is due to the streaming video download not keeping pace with the actual playback of the video. If you find a video stopping and starting, just click the Play/Pause button to pause playback until more of the video has downloaded.

The video itself displays in the main video player window. The playback controls are located directly underneath the main window. From left to right, you use these controls to:

▶ Pause playback by clicking the Play/Pause button; to resume playback, click the Play/Pause button again.

▶ Navigate anywhere within the video by using the slider control. (This control also indicates how much of the video has downloaded; the slider fills with a shaded red color as the video stream downloads.)

▶ View the elapsed and total time for the video via the time display.

▶ Hover over the volume button to display the volume slider (used to control the sound level), or immediately mute the sound by clicking the Volume button.

▶ If the video is available in high-quality (HQ) or high-definition (HD) format, click the appropriate button to display at a higher resolution.

▶ Display the video full screen by clicking the full-screen button; return to normal size by pressing Esc on your computer keyboard.

▶ If closed captioning or annotations are available, click the up arrow button and then select the desired option.

TIP: Full-screen Videos

To watch a video within your web browser, you don't have to do anything other than open the video page. To view the video full-screen (instead of in the browser window) click the full-screen button at the bottom right of the video player.

When a video is done playing, YouTube displays a screen like the one shown in Figure 3.2. Click the Share button to send a link to this video via email to your friends. Click the Replay button to replay the video. Or click one of the other video links to watch a related video.

> **NOTE: Respond**
> Some videos also display a Respond button when they're done playing. Click this button to record your own video response to the video.

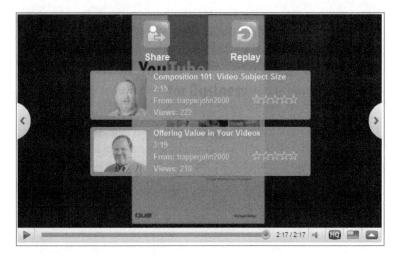

FIGURE 3.2   What you see when a video is done playing.

Viewing Video Information

To the right of the video player is a box with specific information about this video, as shown in Figure 3.3. The information in this box includes:

- ▶ The user who uploaded this video; click the user's name to view his or her YouTube channel

- ▶ When the video was added to YouTube

- ▶ A brief description of the video; click the More Info link to view the complete description

- ▶ The web page URL for this video; copy and paste this URL into your own web page or blog to link back to the video

▶ The HTML code necessary to embed the video in a separate web page or blog; copy and paste this code into your own page to display the video on your website

FIGURE 3.3   Information about a given video.

TIP: **Subscribe**
The information also includes a Subscribe button. Click this button to subscribe to all videos posted by this particular user.

Exploring Related Videos

Below the video information box are other videos you might find interesting (refer to Figure 3.1). Included are More From, which displays other videos uploaded by the same user, and Related Videos, which displays videos in some way similar to this one. In the Related Videos list, click a thumbnail to view one of these videos; scroll to the bottom of each list and click the See All Videos link to view additional videos of this type.

TIP: **Expand the Lists**
The lists of other videos may be contracted (hidden). Click the title of any list to expand it and display all the videos on the list.

Rating the Videos You Watch

Here's another cool thing about YouTube. You can give a rating to any video you've watched. Think a particular video is really hot? Give it a five-star rating. Think a video sucks wind? Then give it a one-star rating. Your voice will be heard.

To rate a video, all you have to do is drag your cursor across the stars beneath the YouTube video player in your web browser; stop your cursor over the star rating you want to give, then click your mouse. You can give a video anywhere from one to five stars—the more stars, the higher the rating. Once you've rated a video, your vote is added to the ratings given by other users to create an overall rating. Thank you for voting!

Reporting Offensive Videos

YouTube is a self-policing community, which means it's your responsibility to report any offending video you might see. Then YouTube can check it out and, if necessary, remove the video from the site.

What do you do if you see a video that violates YouTube's content guidelines—a video that contains nudity or adult language? To report an offending video, click the Flag link in the Options panel directly under the video player. This displays the box shown in Figure 3.4. Pull down the Select a Reason list to tell YouTube what you find offensive about this video:

- ▶ Sexual Content
- ▶ Violent or Repulsive Content
- ▶ Hateful or Abusive Content
- ▶ Harmful Dangerous Acts
- ▶ Spam
- ▶ Infringes My Rights

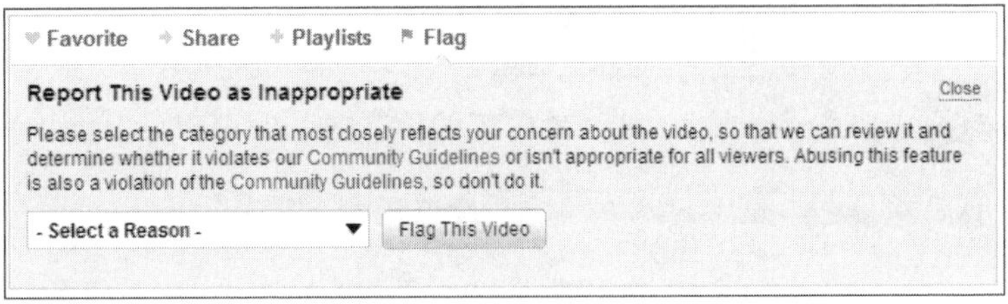

FIGURE 3.4   Reporting an offensive video.

After you make your selection, click the Flag This Video button. Your report is then forwarded to YouTube staffers, who will then investigate the video in question and—if they agree with you—pull the video.

> TIP: **YouTube Decides**
> Just because you report a video as offensive doesn't mean that YouTube will agree with you and pull the video. It's up to YouTube to make content-related decisions like this.

Summary

In this lesson, you learned how to view and rate YouTube videos. In the next lesson, you learn how to view videos in high quality and high definition.

Watching High-Quality and High-Definition Videos

In this lesson, you learn how to watch YouTube's high-quality and high-definition videos.

Understanding Resolution

Whether you're watching on a computer screen or a television display, the quality of a picture is defined by its *resolution*—the number of pixels in the picture. The more pixels, the higher the resolution and the sharper the picture—especially when viewed on larger displays.

> PLAIN ENGLIGH: **Resolution**
>
> The amount of detail in an image. Often measured in terms of pixels; the more pixels, the greater the resolution.

> PLAIN ENGLISH: **Pixel**
>
> The smallest item of information in a digital image; the small dots or squares that compose a digital image.

When YouTube originally launched, all videos were displayed with a relatively low-quality picture. The basic YouTube video player window was only 320 pixels tall × 240 pixels wide, which is about a quarter the resolution of a standard definition television picture. That was good enough for a small video window, but not suitable for broadcast standards.

Over time, YouTube enabled users to upload videos with greater picture resolution. What YouTube aptly calls *high-quality* (HQ) videos have a resolution of 640 × 480 pixels, which is identical to a standard definition television. So you could watch a YouTube HQ video on a standard television set and it would look just like normal television programming.

NOTE: **Widescreen**

Some HQ videos are available in a 16:9 widescreen aspect ratio. These videos have a resolution of 720 × 480 pixels.

Standard definition television is an old technology, however, and is being superseded by new high-definition television (HDTV) broadcasts. HDTV packs more pixels into the picture (a minimum of 1280 × 720) and includes a widescreen display instead of the normal squarish display. (A widescreen display has an aspect ratio of 16:9, while a standard display has a 4:3 aspect ratio.)

PLAIN ENGLISH: **Aspect Ratio**

The aspect ratio describes the width of a display in relation to the display's height. Thus a 16:9 aspect ratio is 16 measures wide by 9 measures tall.

YouTube has embraced this new technology by enabling the upload and playback of high-definition (HD) videos. These videos play back in widescreen at 1280 × 720 resolution, complete with stereo sound.

Of course, to get the full benefit of HQ and HD videos, you need to watch the videos in full-screen mode. You won't see the full detail of an HD picture in YouTube's normal video window; you need to view it larger to display all those extra pixels.

TIP: **Full-screen Mode**

To view a video full-screen on your computer display, click the full-screen button at the lower right of the video window. To return to the normal video window, press the Esc key on your computer keyboard.

Watching High-Quality (HQ) Videos

By default, YouTube displays all its videos in the normal small video window. If a video was uploaded at a higher resolution, you will see an HQ button at the lower-right side of the video window, as shown in Figure 4.1. To display the video at the higher resolution, click the HQ button. This will reload the video at the higher resolution (and turn the HQ button red); you can then choose to watch in the normal video window or go to full-screen mode.

FIGURE 4.1   Click the HQ button to view a video at higher quality.

Watching High-Definition (HD) Videos

If a video is available in high definition, an HD button will be present in the lower-right corner of the video window, as shown in Figure 4.2. To view the video in high definition, click the HD button.

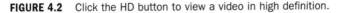

FIGURE 4.2   Click the HD button to view a video in high definition.

This expands the normal video window into a larger HD video window, as shown in Figure 4.3, and turns the HD button red. This window fills up much of the width of your web browser and moves the information box and related videos below the video window. To return to standard definition viewing, click the red HD button.

FIGURE 4.3   Viewing a high-definition (HD) video.

NOTE: **XL Videos**
HD videos look even better on bigger screens. Learn more in Lesson 25, "Watching YouTube XL on Large Displays."

Summary

In this lesson, you learned how to view high quality and high definition videos. In the next lesson, you learn how to manage your favorite videos.

LESSON 5

Saving Your Favorite Videos

In this lesson, you learn how to keep track of your favorite videos.

Creating a QuickList for Future Viewing

Here's a familiar situation. You're browsing the YouTube site and find a video that looks interesting, but you don't have the time or inclination to watch it right now. Fortunately, YouTube lets you save this video in a temporary QuickList, without having to open the video page and start playback. Then, when you're ready, you can go back to this video and watch it at your leisure.

To add a video to your QuickList, all you have to do is click the little "+" button at the lower-left corner of any video thumbnail. Videos stay in your QuickList as long as your web browser is open; as soon as you close your browser window, the QuickList is flushed.

To see all the videos stored in your QuickList, click the QuickList link at the top of any YouTube page. This displays the QuickList page, shown in Figure 5.1. Click any video to view it, or click the Remove button to remove it from your QuickList (in case you decide you don't really want to watch it). You can even play all the videos in your QuickList, one after another, by clicking the Play Quicklist button.

YouTube also places a QuickList panel on all the video pages you open. This panel, shown in Figure 5.2, appears on the left side of the page, between the More Videos and Related Videos lists. You can play individual videos directly from this panel or you can click the Play All link to play all the videos in the QuickList.

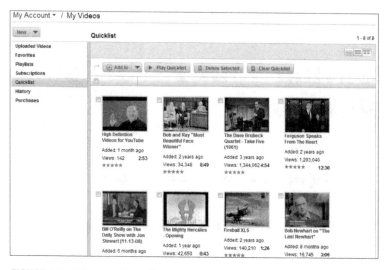

FIGURE 5.1   Viewing videos in your QuickList.

FIGURE 5.2   The QuickList panel on a YouTube video page.

Saving a Favorite Video

When you view a video you really like, you don't want to forget about it. That's why YouTube lets you save your favorite videos in a Favorites list.

PLAIN ENGLISH: **Favorites List**

A YouTube Favorites list is similar to the favorites or bookmarks list you have in your web browser. All your favorite videos are saved in a list which you can easily access for future viewing.

To save a video to your Favorites list, all you have to do is click the Favorite link underneath the video player. This displays a confirmation panel, like the one shown in Figure 5.3.

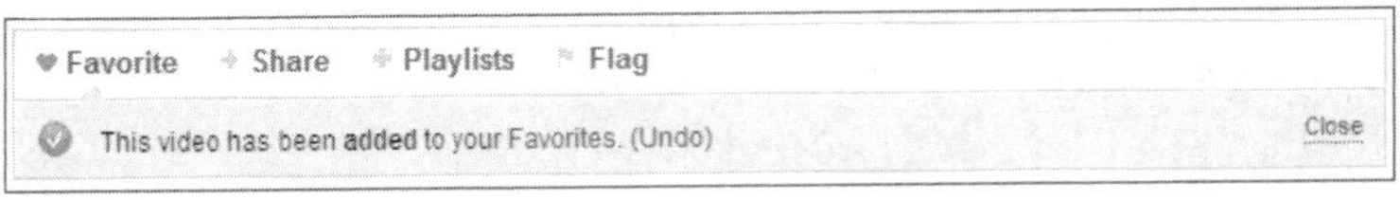

❤ Favorite   ⤳ Share   ✛ Playlists   ⚑ Flag

✓ This video has been added to your Favorites. (Undo)   Close

FIGURE 5.3   Adding a video to your Favorites list.

TIP: **Undo**

If you've added a video to your Favorites list by mistake, click the Undo link in the confirmation panel.

Viewing Your Favorite Videos

When you want to revisit your favorite videos, follow these steps:

1. Click the down arrow next to your user name at the top of any YouTube page and select Favorites.

2. This displays the Favorites page, shown in Figure 5.4. Click any video to watch it again.

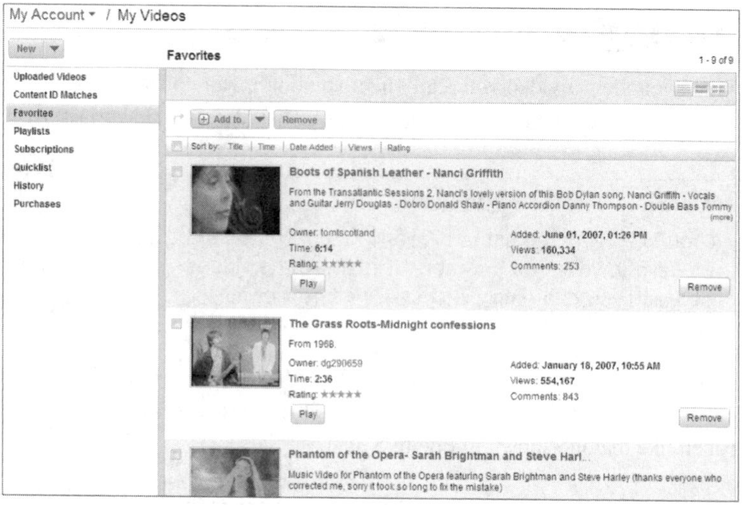

FIGURE 5.4 The videos in your Favorites list.

> TIP: **Undo**
>
> To delete a video from your Favorites list, simply click the Remove button next to that video.

If you have a lot of favorite videos, you can sort the Favorites list by a variety of criteria. Just click one of the following links in the Sort To bar above the list: Title, Time, Date Added, Views, or Rating.

Adding Favorite Videos to a Playlist or QuickList

The Favorites page also enables you to add your favorite videos to a playlist or QuickList. Here's how you do it:

1. On the Favorites page, check the video(s) you want to add to a playlist or QuickList.

2. Click the Add To button and select either Playlist or QuickList.

3. If you selected Playlist, you now see a pane that lists your available playlists. Check the playlist you want to use, then click the Add to Playlist button.

4. If you selected QuickList, the selected video(s) is automatically added to your current QuickList.

> NOTE: **Playlists**
> Learn more about playlists in Lesson 6, "Creating a Video Playlist."

Summary

In this lesson, you learned how to save videos to a QuickList for future viewing and how to save your favorite videos in a Favorites list. In the next lesson, you learn how to create a video playlist.

LESSON 6

Creating a Video Playlist

In this lesson, you learn how to create a playlist of your favorite videos.

Understanding Playlists

One of the problems with YouTube is the sheer volume of videos available. Saving videos to your Favorites list is one way to manage this volume, but even your Favorites list can get too large to be easily manageable.

For that reason, you may want to create *playlists* separate from (or in addition to) your Favorites list. A YouTube playlist is simply a collection of videos, organized by whatever criteria you deem appropriate. You can play the videos in a playlist individually or as a group, just as you would the songs in a music playlist on your iPod. And, of course, YouTube lets you create multiple playlists, so you can have as many as you like.

> PLAIN ENGLISH: **Playlist**
> A collection of videos that can be played individually or as a group.

Creating a Playlist from a Video Page

To create a new playlist, you start with the first video you want in the playlist. Follow these steps:

1. Open the page for the video you want to add to the playlist.

2. Click the Playlists link underneath the video window.

3. The Add to Playlist area now appears. Select [New Playlist] from the list and click the Add button.

4. This displays the Create/Edit Playlist page, shown in Figure 6.1. Enter a name and description for the playlist, as well as any tags you want to use to describe the playlist.

PLAIN ENGLISH: **Tag**

A keyword used to describe the contents of a video.

NOTE: **Video Log**

YouTube used to let users include a list of selected videos, called a *video log*, on their channel pages. While this feature is no longer available, references to it remain in places on the YouTube site—including on the Create/Edit Playlist page.

---

5. Still on the Create/Edit Playlist page, select whether you want the playlist to be Public (displayed to other users on your Profile page) or Private (not visible to others).

6. If you want other users to be able to display your playlist on their websites, check the Allow External Sites to Embed This Playlist option. If you'd rather not have your playlist publicized in this fashion, do not check this option.

7. Click the Save Playlist Info button. Your new playlist is now created and saved.

Once you've filled in all the blanks, click the Save Playlist Info button. Your playlist is now saved.

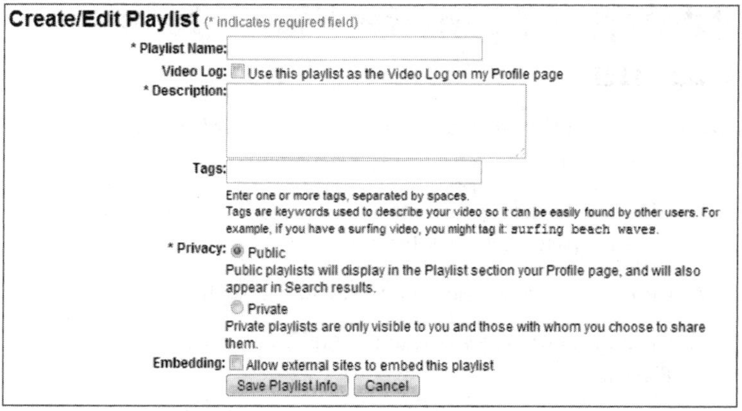

Create/Edit Playlist (* indicates required field)

* Playlist Name: [_____]

Video Log: ☐ Use this playlist as the Video Log on my Profile page

* Description: [_____]

Tags: [_____]

Enter one or more tags, separated by spaces.

Tags are keywords used to describe your video so it can be easily found by other users. For example, if you have a surfing video, you might tag it: surfing beach waves.

* Privacy: ◉ Public

Public playlists will display in the Playlist section your Profile page, and will also appear in Search results.

◯ Private

Private playlists are only visible to you and those with whom you choose to share them.

Embedding: ☐ Allow external sites to embed this playlist

[Save Playlist Info] [Cancel]

FIGURE 6.1   Creating a new playlist.

Adding a Video to a Playlist

There are several ways to add a video to an existing playlist. The most common method is to add the video to your playlist from the video page itself. Follow these steps:

1. Open the page for the video you want to add.

2. Click the Playlists link underneath the video window.

3. The Add to Playlist area appears, as shown in Figure 6.2. Select the playlist you want from the list and click the Add button.

♥ Favorite   → Share   + Playlists   ⚑ Flag

Add to Playlist   Close

[Jazz (6 videos) ▼] [Add]

FIGURE 6.2   Adding a video to a playlist.

Adding a Favorite Video to a Playlist

Another way to add a video to a playlist is from your Favorites list. Follow these steps:

1. Click the down arrow next to your username at the top of any YouTube page, then click Favorites.

2. Check the video(s) you want to add to the playlist.

3. Click the down arrow next to the Add To button and select Playlist.

4. When the Add the Selected Videos To box appears, as shown in Figure 6.3, check the desired playlist and click the Add to Playlist button.

FIGURE 6.3   Adding a Favorite video to a playlist.

Viewing Video Playlists

To view and play back the playlists you've created, follow these steps:

1. Click the down arrow next to your username at the top of any YouTube page, then click Playlists.

2. This displays the Playlists page, shown in Figure 6.4. Select a playlist from the Playlists section on the left side of the page.

3. This displays all the videos in the selected playlist. To play all the videos in the playlist, click the Play All button. To play an individual video in the playlist, click the thumbnail for that video.

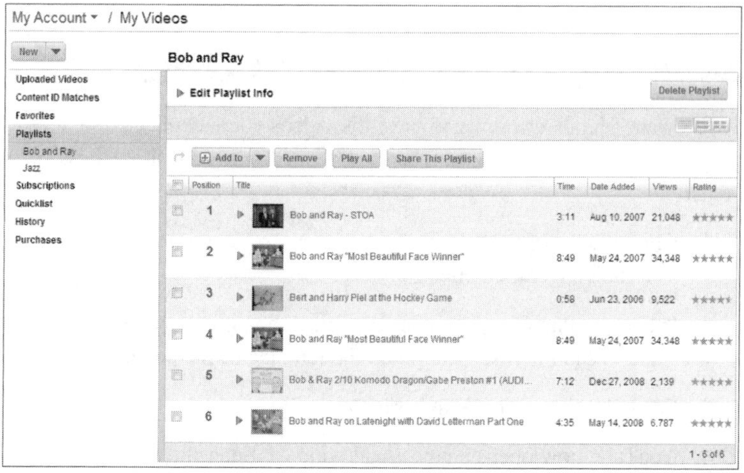

FIGURE 6.4 Viewing your YouTube playlists.

Editing Your Playlists

You can also use the Playlists page to edit the videos in your playlists—and the playlists themselves. Follow these steps:

1. Click the down arrow next to your username at the top of any YouTube page, then click Playlists.

2. When the Playlists page appears, select the playlist you want to edit in the Playlists section on the left side of the page.

3. To change the order of playback in a playlist, enter new numbers to the left of each video; click a number to change it. The "1" video plays first, the "2" video plays second, and so on.

4. To remove a video from a playlist, check the video and then click the Remove button.

5. To edit the title or description of a playlist, click the Edit Playlist Info link to expand the top of the page. Change any information you want, then click the Save Changes button.

6. To delete an entire playlist, click the Delete Playlist button.

Sharing a Playlist with Others

If you want friends or family to view the videos you've collected in a playlist, you can share your playlist with them. To do so, follow these steps:

1. Click the down arrow next to your username at the top of any YouTube page, then click Playlists.

2. When the Playlists page appears, select the playlist you want to share in the Playlists section on the left side of the page.

3. Click the Share This Playlist button.

4. YouTube now opens a new email window. Enter the email addresses of the people you want to share with into the Email To: box (separated by commas); enter an optional personal message into the Add a Personal Message box; then click the Send button.

Your friends will receive an email from YouTube that contains a link to this playlist. When they click the link, they'll be taken to the YouTube site to view the videos in the playlist.

Summary

In this lesson, you learned how to create new playlists, save videos to a playlist, and edit and share a playlist. In the next lesson, you learn how to subscribe to videos from your favorite users.

LESSON 7

Subscribing to Videos

In this lesson, you learn how to subscribe to videos from YouTube users.

Understanding Channels and Subscriptions

On YouTube, each user has his own channel. Your channel shows all the videos you've uploaded, just as a television or cable channel shows its distinctive programming.

> **PLAIN ENGLISH: Channel**
>
> A user's home page on the YouTube site. A channel includes all the videos uploaded by a given user, as well as that user's Favorite videos.

You can visit a user's channel by clicking on that person's user name on any video page. You'll find the user's name in the information box to the right of the video viewing window.

If you like the videos uploaded by a given user, you can *subscribe* to that person's channel. When you subscribe to a channel, you are periodically notified (via email) when the user uploads new videos. It's a great way to keep current on the kinds of videos you like.

Subscribing to a User's Videos

The easiest way to subscribe to a user's channel is to go to the page for one of that user's videos. The information box above or next to the video has a big yellow Subscribe button, as shown in Figure 7.1; click this button to subscribe to that user's videos.

FIGURE 7.1   Click the Subscribe button to subscribe to this user's videos.

You can also subscribe to a user from that user's channel page. To go to the user's channel page, click the person's user name on any video page. You can then click the Subscribe button on that page, typically located near the top of the page, as shown in Figure 7.2.

Michael Miller's Videos   Subscribe   **All**   **Uploads**   **Favorites**
trapperjohn2000's Channel

FIGURE 7.2   Subscribing to a user's videos from his channel page.

Managing Your Subscriptions

To manage your YouTube subscriptions, follow these steps:

1. Click the down arrow next to your username at the top of any YouTube page, then select Subscriptions.

2. When the next page appears, as shown in Figure 7.3, all your subscriptions are listed in the Subscriptions list on the left side of the page. Click a user name to view the most recent videos from that user.

3. To unsubscribe from a user's channels, select that user in the Subscriptions list and then click the Unsubscribe button.

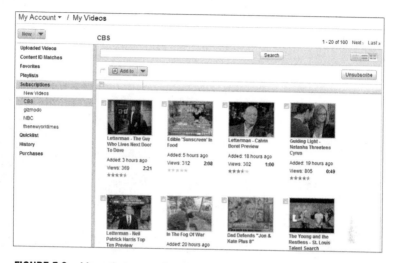

FIGURE 7.3 Managing your subscriptions from the Subscriptions page.

Summary

In this lesson, you learned how to subscribe to user videos. In the next lesson, you learn how to share videos with others via email.

LESSON 8

Sharing a YouTube Video via Email

In this lesson, you learn how to share your favorite videos with friends and family.

Sharing an Individual Video

If you like a video, chances are you have a friend who'll like that video, too. That's why YouTube lets you share the videos you like—in fact, this type of video sharing is one of the defining features of the whole YouTube experience.

You share YouTube videos via email, sent through the YouTube system. Follow these steps:

1. Go to the page for the video you want to share.

2. Click the Share link underneath the video player window. This expands the Share section.

3. Scroll to the Send This Video from YouTube section, shown in Figure 8.1.

4. Enter the email addresses of the intended recipients into the To box.

5. Enter an optional personal message into the Message box.

6. Click the Send button.

> TIP: **Multiple Recipients**
> To share a video with multiple people, separate multiple email addresses with commas.

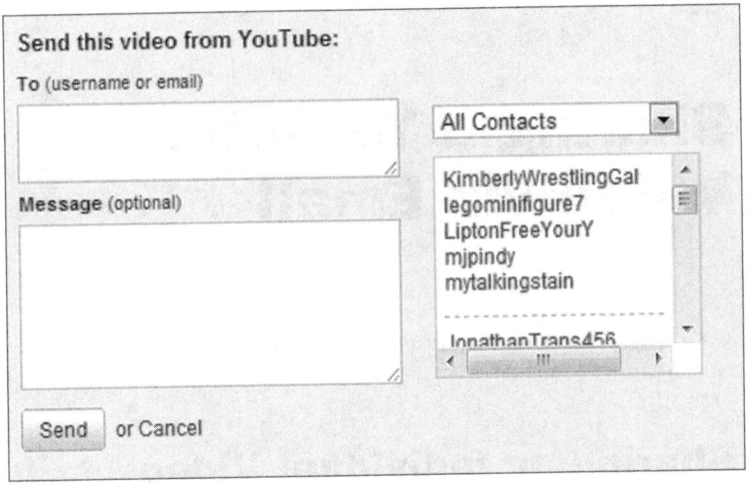

FIGURE 8.1 Sharing a video via email.

The message your friends receive looks like the one shown in Figure 8.2. To view the video, they simply click the video thumbnail or link. This opens a web browser, accesses the YouTube site, and starts playing the video you shared.

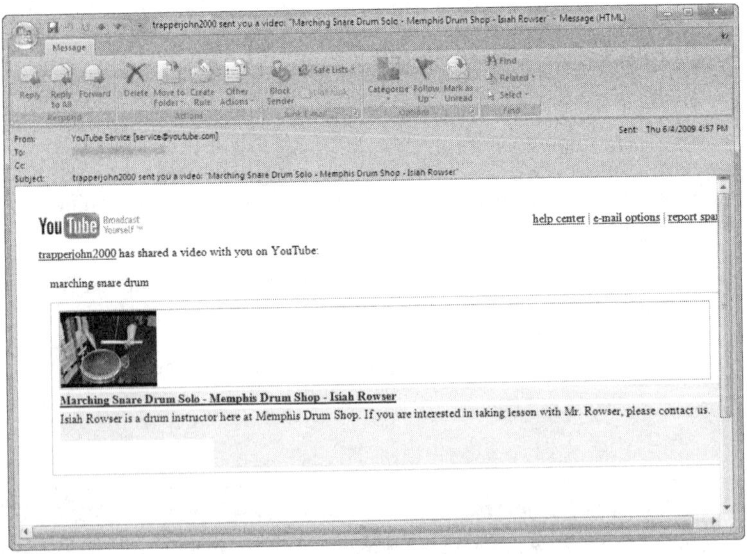

FIGURE 8.2 An email invitation to view a YouTube video.

Sharing a Playlist

YouTube also lets you share complete playlists with your friends. To do so, follow these steps:

1. Click the down arrow next to your username at the top of any YouTube page, then select Playlists.

2. When the Playlists page appears, as shown in Figure 8.3, select a playlist from the list on the left side of the page.

3. Click the Share This Playlist button.

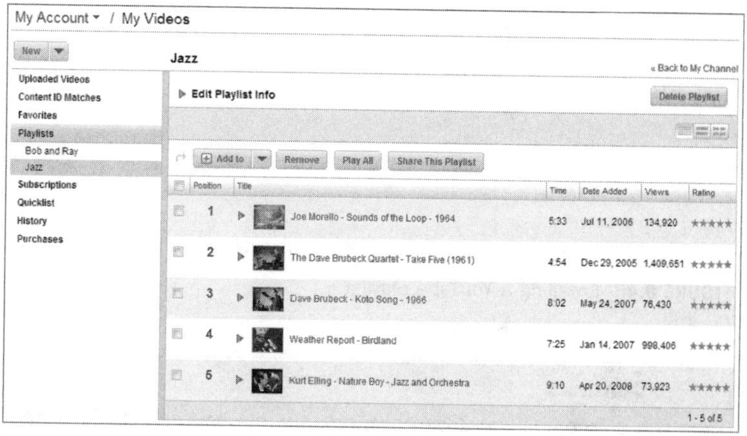

FIGURE 8.3 Sharing a playlist.

4. You now see an email window, as shown in Figure 8.4. Enter the email addresses of the intended recipients into the Email To box.

5. Enter an optional personal message into the Add a Personal Message box.

6. Click the Send button.

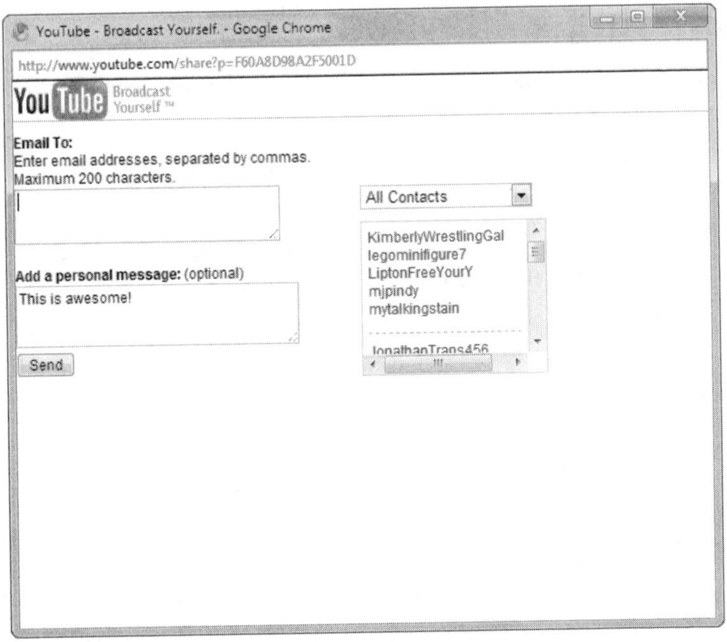

FIGURE 8.4   Emailing a YouTube playlist.

NOTE: **Contacts**

You can also email your favorite videos and playlists directly to users you've added to your YouTube contacts list. Learn more about YouTube emailing in Lesson 24, "Communicating with Other YouTube Users."

Summary

In this lesson, you learned how to email links to your favorite videos to friends and family. In the next lesson, you learn how to link to YouTube videos in email messages, blogs, and websites.

Linking to and Embedding YouTube Videos

In this lesson, you learn how to include links to videos and embed videos in your website and email messages.

Linking to a YouTube Video

Another way to share a YouTube video is to pass around a link to that video. You can include video links in your email messages, as well as on your own blog or web page. You can even link to YouTube videos from Facebook and MySpace.

YouTube makes it easy to link to its videos. Every video page has its own URL and includes a snippet of HTML code you can insert to create a link to the page.

To link to a specific YouTube video, follow these steps:

1. Go to the page for the video you want to link to.

2. A URL box (shown in Figure 9.1) is in the information box to the right of the video. Highlight and copy the HTML code in this box.

3. Paste that HTML code into your email message, blog post, or body of your web page.

FIGURE 9.1   Copy the URL from the information box into your email message, blog post, or web page.

Anyone reading your email, blog, or web page can then click this link and be taken to the video viewing page on the YouTube site.

If you're copying the link into a web page, make sure you surround it with the appropriate HTML link tag. The resulting code should look something like this:

```
Click <a href="http://www.youtube.com/watch?v=12345">here</a>
to view my YouTube video.
```

Naturally, replace the href link with the URL from the video you're linking to.

> **NOTE: HTML**
> To paste a YouTube link on your web page, you must have access to and be familiar with basic HTML commands.

Embedding a YouTube Video in Your Website

Linking to YouTube videos from your web page is one thing; embedding an actual video into your web page or blog is quite another. That's right—YouTube lets you insert any of its public videos into your own web page, complete with a video player window. And it's easy to do.

YouTube automatically creates the embed code for every public video on its site and lists this code on the video page itself. The code is in the information box beside the video, as you saw in Figure 9.1; you'll need to copy this entire code (it's longer than the Embed box itself) and then paste it into the HTML code on your own web page. Just follow these steps:

1. Go to the page for the video you want to link to.

2. In the information box to the left of the video is an Embed box. Highlight and copy the HTML code in this box.

3. Paste that HTML code into your web page's underlying HTML code where you want the embedded video to appear.

The result of inserting this code into your page's HTML is that your web page now displays a special click-to-play YouTube video player window, like the one shown in Figure 9.2. The video itself remains stored on and served from YouTube's servers; only the code resides on your website. When a site visitor clicks the video, it's served from YouTube's servers to your viewer's web browser, just as if it were served from your own server. (This means you don't waste any of your own storage space or bandwidth on the video.)

FIGURE 9.2   A YouTube video embedded in a web page.

By the way, the code in the Embed box is squished together onto a single line to make it easier to copy. If you were to properly format the code, it would look something like this:

```
<object width="425" height="350">
   <param name="movie"
value="http://www.youtube.com/v/12345"></param>
   <param name="wmode" value="transparent"></param>
   <embed src="http://www.youtube.com/v/12345"
   type="application/x-shockwave-flash" wmode="transparent"
width="425"
   height="350">
   </embed>
</object>
```

CAUTION: **Don't Use This Code**
Don't copy *this* code to your web page—it's just an example!

Customizing an Embedded Video

There are a few options you can choose that affect how an embedded video looks on your web page. You access these options by clicking the Customize button next to the Embed box on the original video page, as shown in Figure 9.3. These options include the following:

► **Include related videos.** Check this option to display related videos when the embedded video is done playing; uncheck this option to not show related videos.

► **Show Border**. Check this option to put a border around the embedded video player.

► **Enable delayed cookies**. The title of this option is a little confusing, but in essence when this option is selected, YouTube doesn't leave cookies on viewers' computers—which is better for viewers' security.

► **Color scheme**. Choose from seven different color schemes for the embedded video player.

▶ **Size**. Choose from four different sizes for the embedded video player. For standard aspect videos, the available sizes are 320 × 265 , 425 × 344, 480 × 385, and 640 ×505 (HQ pixels). For widescreen videos, the available sizes are 480 × 295, 560 × 340, 640 × 385, and 853 × 505 (HD pixels).

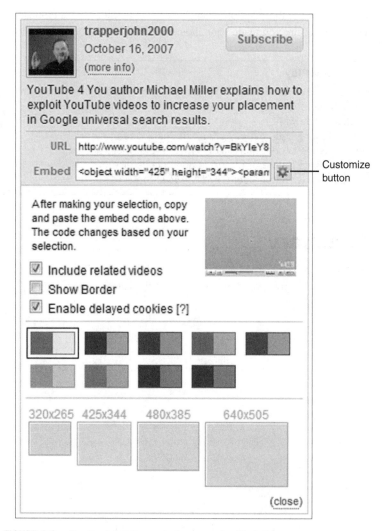

Customize button

FIGURE 9.3   Customizing the code for an embedded video.

> PLAIN ENGLISH: **Cookie**
>
> A small file left on a user's computer by a website that tracks the user's activities on that website. YouTube typically leaves cookies that track viewing history and the like.

Choosing any of these options changes the HTML code for the embedded video. Make sure you made your choices *before* copying the embed code.

> TIP: **Auto Play**
>
> By default, an embedded video doesn't play automatically when your web page loads; visitors have to click the Play button to view the video. If you want the video to play automatically, you have to insert the following code directly after both instances of the video's URL in the embed code: **&autoplay=1**. Note that there should be no space before or after this added code, like this: **http://www.youtube.com/v/12345&autoplay=1**.

Summary

In this lesson, you learned how to link to and embed YouTube videos. In the next lesson, you learn how to post YouTube videos to your blog.

Posting a YouTube Video to Your Blog

In this lesson, you learn to post videos from YouTube to your own blog.

Configuring YouTube for Blog Posting

If you have your own personal blog on the web, YouTube makes it easy to send any public YouTube video to your blog as a blog posting. The video appears in new blog post, along with any text you enter to accompany the video.

> PLAIN ENGLISH: **Blog**
> Short for "web log," a website that enables personal commentary from the blog's owner. Kind of like a web-based diary.

To post videos to your blog, you first have to configure YouTube to work with your blog, so it knows where to send your posts. To do this, follow these steps:

1. Click the Account link at the top of any YouTube page.

2. When the My Account page appears, click the Blog Setup link on the left side of the page.

3. When the Blog Setup page appears, as shown in Figure 10.1, click the Add a Blog button.

4. When the Add a Blog/Site box appears, as shown in Figure 10.2, pull down the Blog Service list and select your blog host.

5. Enter the email/username and password you use to access your blog.

6. Click the Add Blog button.

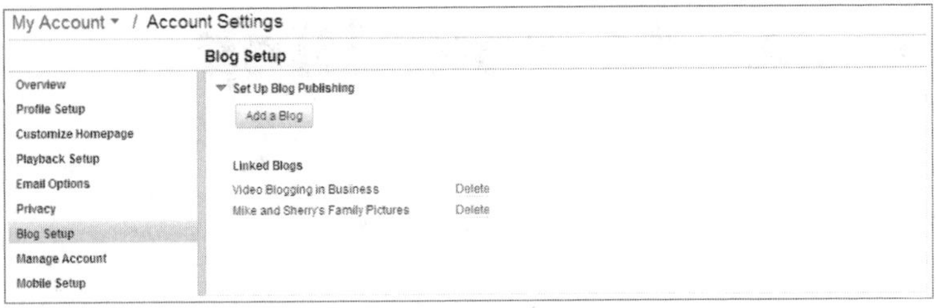

FIGURE 10.1   Click the Blog Setup link to display the Add a Blog button.

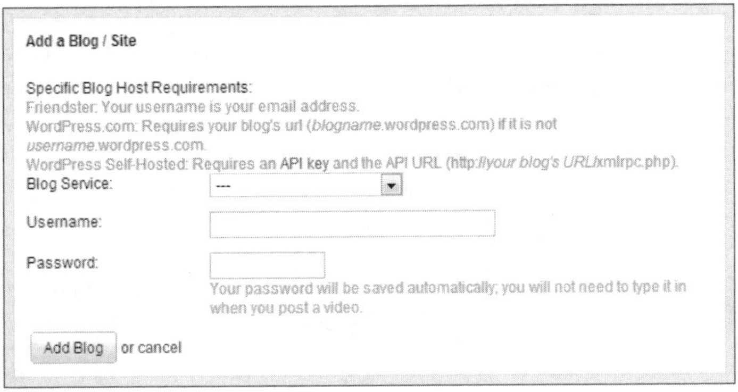

FIGURE 10.2   Configuring YouTube for blog posting.

If you have more than one blog at a given host, you'll now see a list of all your blogs. Check those you want to post to, then click the Add Selected Blogs button.

NOTE: **Supported Blogs**

YouTube supports automatic posting to the following blog hosts: Blogger, FreeWebs, Friendster, LiveJournal, Piczo, WordPress.com, and WordPress self-hosted blogs. To add blogs from different hosts, repeat the numbered steps for each blog host.

Posting a Video

Once configured, it's a snap to send any public YouTube video to your blog—including videos you've uploaded and those others have uploaded. Here's how to do it:

1. Go to the page for the video you want to post.

2. Click the Share link under the video; this expands the panel under the video, as shown in Figure 10.3.

3. Pull down the Blog list and select your blog.

4. Enter a title for this post into the Title box.

5. Enter any text you want to accompany the video post into the Text box.

6. Click the Post to Blog button.

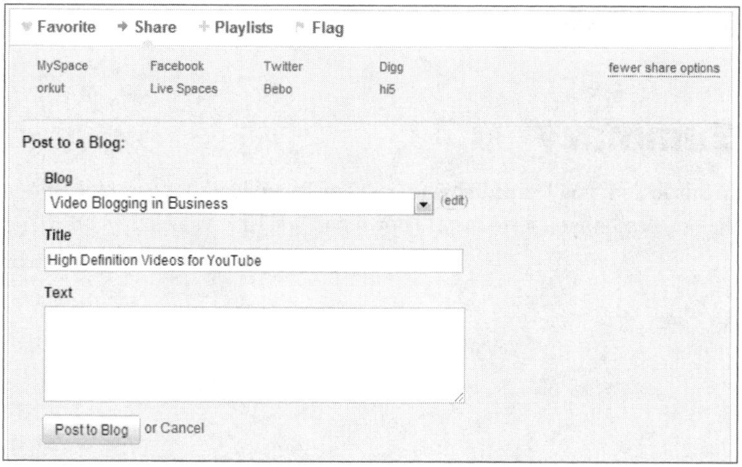

FIGURE 10.3   Posting a video to your blog.

YouTube now posts the video (and accompanying text) to your blog as a new post. (Figure 10.4 shows a typical blog with YouTube videos added.) It's that easy!

FIGURE 10.4   Posting a video to your blog.

Summary

In this lesson, you learned how to post YouTube videos to your blog. In the next lesson, you learn how to download YouTube videos to your PC.

Downloading YouTube Videos

In this lesson, you learn how to download YouTube videos to your computer or portable device.

Why Downloading Isn't an Official Option—Yet

As you learned in Lesson 1, "Getting to Know YouTube," YouTube is a streaming video service. That means that it streams its videos from its site to your computer screen. You don't actually download and save the videos to your computer; the videos are streamed in real time to your web browser using the Adobe Flash Player.

The problem with the streaming video approach is that the videos you watched aren't saved to your PC's hard drive; if you want to watch a video when you're not connected to the Internet, you can't.

Until YouTube adds downloading to its list of viewing options (which it is in the process of testing), the solution to this dilemma is to use a third-party program or website to download YouTube's streaming videos to video files on your computer's hard drive. There are several programs and sites that perform this service; we'll show you how to use the best of these next.

> NOTE: **Partner Videos**
> YouTube currently offers downloading of videos from some of its high-volume commercial users, so-called partners. Many of these partners charge for downloading their videos.

Downloading to Your Computer with RealPlayer

The best and easiest-to-use software program for downloading YouTube videos is the latest version of RealPlayer (www.real.com/player/). This is a free program that enables one-button downloading of any video from the YouTube site—and also functions as a player for .FLV-format videos (among others).

> NOTE: **Flash**
>
> YouTube's videos are served in Adobe's Flash video format, with an .FLV file extension.

Downloading a Video

When you install RealPlayer, you also install a special add-in for Internet Explorer and other web browsers. This add-in automatically displays a Download This Video button above the top right corner of any video you view on the YouTube site, as shown in Figure 11.1.

FIGURE 11.1   Click the Download This Video button to download the video for RealPlayer playback.

TIP: **Download from Other Sites**

RealPlayer displays the same Download This Video button on any video streaming site, so you can download videos from any website that offers streaming videos.

To download a YouTube video, follow these steps:

1. Go to the YouTube page for the video you want to download.

2. Hover your cursor over the video window to display the Download This Video button.

3. Click the Download This Video button.

4. RealPlayer displays the Download & Recording Manager window and automatically saves the video to your hard drive.

NOTE: **Displaying the Button**

You don't have to have the RealPlayer program running to display the Download This Video button in your web browser. The button is an add-in program that launches automatically whenever you launch your web browser.

That's all you have to do; the video file is automatically named and saved to your hard drive.

Playing a Downloaded Video

You use the RealPlayer program to play back all the YouTube videos you've downloaded. To play back a video, follow these steps:

1. From within RealPlayer, select the My Library tab, shown in Figure 11.2; this displays all the videos you've downloaded.

2. Double-click a video to start playback.

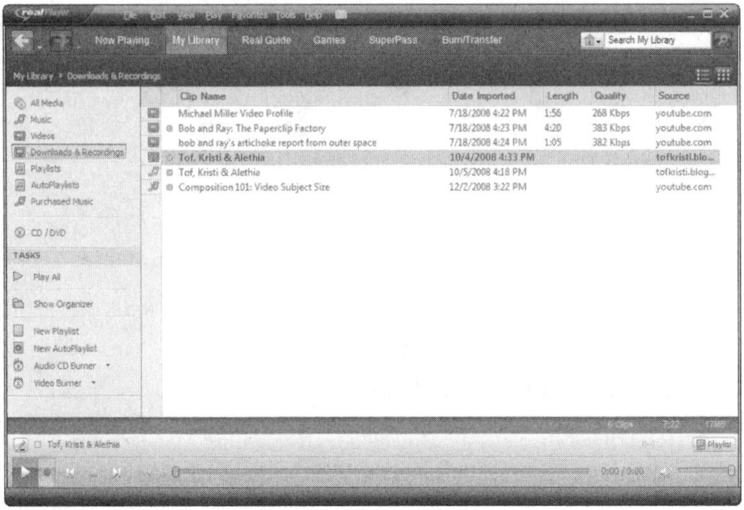

FIGURE 11.2   YouTube videos in your RealPlayer library.

Video playback starts in a new RealPlayer window, as shown in Figure 11.3. You can now use RealPlayer's transport controls to pause, stop, rewind, and fast-forward the video.

FIGURE 11.3   Viewing a downloaded YouTube video in RealPlayer.

Downloading to Your iPod

If you have an Apple iPod with video playback, you can download
YouTube videos to your iPod or Sony PSP for playback on the go. To do
this, however, you must both download a YouTube streaming video and
convert it to the MPEG-4 file format used by the iPod and PSP.

> NOTE: **MPEG-4**
>
> MPEG-4 video files have either an .MP4 or .MPV extension.

There are several software programs available to convert downloaded
FLV-format YouTube videos to the MPEG-4 file format. That said, the
easiest way to download and convert YouTube videos for iPod/PSP use is
to use the vixy.net Online FLV Converter. This is a website, located at
http://vixy.net, that downloads and converts any YouTube video to
iPod/PSP video format, with no software necessary. The service is free.

To use vixy.net, follow these steps:

1. Go to the YouTube page for the video you want to download.

2. Copy the video's URL from the URL box in the information
   box.

3. Go to vixy.net (www.vixy.net).

4. Paste the URL for the video into the URL box, shown in Figure
   11.4.

5. Pull down the Converts To list and select MP4 for iPod/PSP
   (MPEG4 + AAC).

6. Click the Start button.

7. The website now converts the video. When the Save As dialog
   box appears, browse to the directory where your iPod or PSP
   files are stored and then click the Save button.

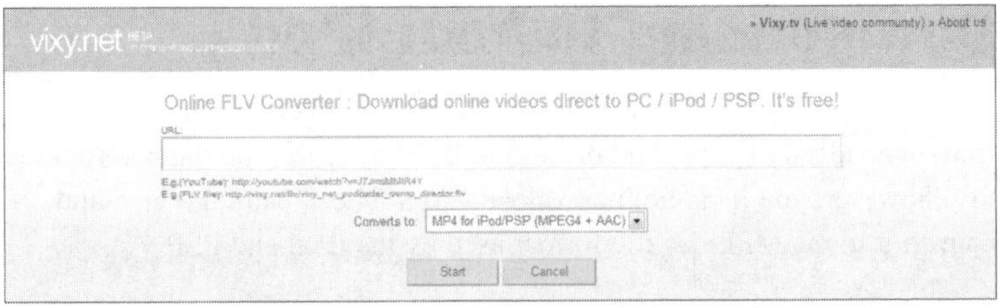

FIGURE 11.4   Converting and downloading a YouTube file with vixy.net.

> NOTE: **Viewing on an iPhone**
>
> If you have an Apple iPhone or iPod Touch, you can view YouTube videos online, no downloading necessary. Learn more in Lesson 12, "Watching YouTube Videos on Your iPhone."

Downloading Your Own Videos

While YouTube doesn't yet let you download other users' videos, you can download your own videos. This is a good thing if you accidentally delete a video from your own computer; you can use YouTube as a kind of online backup service!

To download one of your own videos, follow these steps:

1. Click the down arrow next to your user name at the top of any YouTube page, then select My Videos.

2. When the My Videos page appears, click the Download MP4 button next to the video you want to download, as shown in Figure 11.5.

3. When the Save As window appears, select a location for the download and then click the Save button.

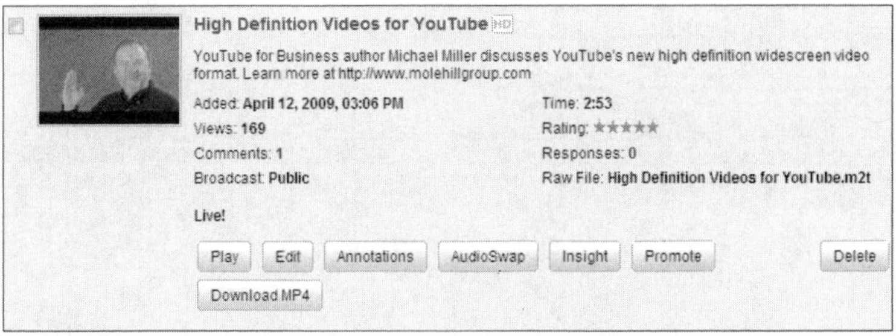

FIGURE 11.5 Downloading your own video from the YouTube site.

YouTube downloads the video in the MPEG-4 format, with an .MP4 file extension. You can then play the video on your computer using any video player program, such as Windows Media Player.

Summary

In this lesson, you learned how to download YouTube videos to your computer, iPod, and PSP. In the next lesson, you learn how to play YouTube videos in real-time on your Apple iPhone or iPod Touch.

Watching YouTube Videos on Your iPhone

In this lesson, you learn how to use the iPhone's YouTube application.

Searching for Videos on Your iPhone

The Apple iPhone is one of the most popular mobile phones today. Its popularity is due in no small part to its ability to access the Internet via either WiFi or a fast 3G cellular connection. This ability to browse the web anytime, anywhere also enables you to view any YouTube video wherever you may happen to be.

> **NOTE: iPod Touch**
>
> The iPod Touch has the same Internet features (and YouTube application) as the iPhone, but without the mobile phone feature.

Apple builds a YouTube application right into the iPhone; it's available from the iPhone's main screen. You can use this application to browse, search for, and play YouTube videos, whether your iPhone is connected via WiFi or a 3G cellular network.

To access and search YouTube from your iPhone, follow these steps:

1. From the iPhone's main screen, tap the YouTube icon.

2. When the YouTube application opens, tap the Search icon at the bottom of the screen.

3. When the search box appears at the top of the iPhone screen, tap the search box to display the iPhone keyboard, as shown in Figure 12.1.

4. Enter your query and tap the Search button.

5. Videos that match your query are now displayed on the Search screen, as shown in Figure 12.2. Tap any thumbnail to view that video.

FIGURE 12.1   Entering a search query on the iPhone.

NOTE: **Signing In**

When you first access YouTube from your iPhone, you'll be asked to sign into your account. Enter your user name and password as requested.

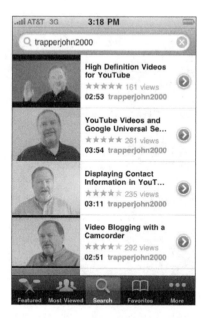

FIGURE 12.2   Viewing search results on the iPhone.

Displaying Your Favorite Videos on Your iPhone

You can also access videos on your Favorites list from your iPhone. Follow these steps:

1. From within the YouTube application, tap the Favorites icon at the bottom of the screen.

2. When your Favorites list appears, as shown in Figure 12.3, tap the right arrow next to any video to display a page for that video, along with related videos. To view more information about that video, including comments left by other users, tap the right arrow on this second page; this displays the page shown in Figure 12.4.

3. To view any video on your Favorites list, tap the thumbnail image for that video.

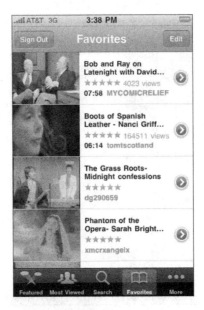

FIGURE 12.3   Viewing your Favorites list.

FIGURE 12.4   Viewing information about a video.

Other Ways to Find Videos on Your iPhone

The YouTube application for the iPhone features several other ways to find videos on the YouTube site. You can do the following:

- ▶ View today's featured videos—tap the Featured icon

- ▶ View the today's most viewed videos—tap the Most Viewed icon

- ▶ View YouTube's newest videos—tap the More icon, then tap the Most Recent icon

- ▶ View the highest-rated videos—tap the More icon, then tap the Top Rated icon

- ▶ Display a history of the videos you've watched—tap the More icon, then tap the History icon

- ▶ Display all the videos you've uploaded—tap the More icon, then tap the My Videos icon

- ▶ Display a list of your channel subscriptions—tap the More icon, then tap the Subscriptions icon

- ▶ Display your video playlists—tap the More icon, then tap the Playlists icon

Viewing Videos on Your iPhone

YouTube videos on the iPhone are displayed in widescreen mode, which means you have to turn your iPhone sideways to view them. To display the transport controls, shown in Figure 12.5, you first have to tap the screen; the transport controls are then overlaid on the video. Tap the screen again to hide the controls.

FIGURE 12.5   Viewing a YouTube video on the iPhone.

To pause a video, tap the Pause/Play control; tap this control again to resume playback. You can also fast forward or reverse through a video by pressing the controls on either side of the Pause/Play control, or by dragging the slider at the top of the screen.

To add this video to your Favorites list, tap the Favorites icon (the open book). To email a link to this video, tap the Email icon (the envelope); when the email message screen appears, enter the recipient's email address and tap the Send button.

> TIP: **Zooming**
> To zoom into a standard aspect ratio, to make it fill the full width of the iPod screen, tap the Full Screen icon at the top right of the screen. Tap this icon again to return to normal viewing size.

Summary

In this lesson, you learned how to watch YouTube videos on your iPhone or iPod Touch. In the next lesson, you learn how to shoot your own videos for the YouTube site.

LESSON 13
Shooting Videos for YouTube

In this lesson, you learn how to shoot a YouTube video.

Shooting with a Webcam

There are three ways to record a video for YouTube. If you have a big budget, you can go with a professional recording, complete with lights, sound, pro-grade video cameras, and the like—although few YouTube videos have this type of over-the-top production. More common—and less costly—are videos shot with a consumer grade camcorder. And if even that sounds pricey to you, you can record your videos with a standard computer webcam, like the one shown in Figure 13.1.

> PLAIN ENGLISH: **Webcam**
> A small camera, typically with accompanying miniature microphone, that attaches to any computer via USB port. Most webcams are designed to fit on top of your monitor screen; some notebook PCs come with a webcam built in.

FIGURE 13.1   Logitech's QuickCam Pro 9000 webcam.
(Photo courtesy Logitech.)

Pros and Cons of Webcam Videos

Given the webcam's small footprint, it makes for a relatively unobtrusive
way to shoot YouTube videos. Also, when attached to a notebook PC
operating on battery power, a webcam lets you shoot videos anywhere
you can take your notebook—a truly portable solution.

Webcams, however, do not produce the highest quality video and audio.
The typical low-priced webcam shoots video at a resolution of 640 × 480,
but has a low-quality lens that doesn't work well in darkened conditions
and doesn't produce especially sharp images. Higher-priced webcams,
such as Logitech's QuickCam Pro 9000, can capture images at 1600 ×
1200 high-definition resolution, and also include a higher-quality lens—
albeit without a zoom feature. Still, if you want broadcast-quality video, a
webcam is the least satisfactory of the different shooting options.

The audio you get with a webcam also leaves much to be desired. In most
instances, you'll be speaking into a small microphone embedded within
the webcam itself; the farther away you are from the webcam, the less
clear your voice will sound when users listen to your video. And, let's be

honest, this isn't studio-quality audio here; webcam audio is barely satisfactory for voice, and really doesn't cut it for much of anything else.

That said, the lower-quality picture and sound inherent with webcam capture lends your webcam videos a sense of immediacy; the effect is one of
raw, "you are there" citizen journalism. The effect is also one of direct-
ness, a one-on-one communication between the speaker and the viewer,
with little in the way of fancy production in between.

Shooting a Webcam Video

Webcam videos are easy to make. You just have to turn on your computer's webcam, launch the webcam software, and press the record button.
You're now recording, until you press the record or stop button.

Everything you record should be saved to a video file on your hard drive.
You can then upload this raw file to YouTube or edit it first using a video
editing program.

> NOTE: **Uploading Live**
>
> YouTube also lets you upload webcam videos live, as you record
> them. Learn more in Lesson 15, "Uploading a Video to YouTube."

Shooting with a Camcorder

While shooting with a webcam is both easy and low cost, you'll get much
better results using a consumer-grade camcorder. We're talking the kinds
of video camcorders you can find at your local Best Buy, augmented by
sophisticated video-editing software and the appropriate accessories. The
resulting videos can look almost identical to professionally made
videos—but without expensive professional involvement.

Choosing a Camcorder

You don't have to spend a lot of money to buy a camcorder today. As it
always does, developing technology helps to bring you better performance

at a significantly lower price than you would have paid just a few years ago. The challenge is picking the right camcorder for your needs.

At the low end of the camcorder range is something called the "flip" camera. These camcorders, like the Flip Video models (shown in Figure 13.2) and the Sony Webbie, are pocket-sized camcorders that are little more than portable webcams. They have similar resolution, features, and picture quality as PC webcams, but don't have to be tethered to a computer to work. Instead, they capture video using built-in flash memory or external memory cards. The Flip Video units have a built-in USB connector so you can plug the camera itself right into your PC's USB port for file transfer; with the Sony models, you remove the memory card and insert it into your computer's memory card reader.

FIGURE 13.2   The Flip Video Ultra—a low-priced camcorder alternative. (Photo courtesy Flip Video.)

Standard definition flip cameras are priced in the $150 range, while high definition units sell for about $200. Know, however, that since these types of camcorders don't have fancy lenses (and, in many cases, little or no zoom capability), they're best suited for talking head videos, just like webcams are.

For the best performance, however, you need to move up to a traditional camcorder, like the one shown in Figure 13.3. These camcorders are suitable for all sorts of videos, from simple vlogs to more demanding how-to shots. Even the lowest price traditional camcorder will take surprisingly good pictures; most of the picture quality is in the file format itself, rather than in the additional features in a particular camcorder. This means that many people can get by with a simple $250 camcorder, no problem. But higher-priced models are available and worthy of your consideration.

FIGURE 13.3   JVC's affordable GZ-MG330 hard-disk camcorder. (Photo courtesy JVC.)

The more money you spend on a camcorder, the more bells and whistles you get. In particular, a bigger budget typically buys you one or more of the following: compact size, ease of use, a bigger zoom lens, special features (such as transition effects, night-vision shooting, and so on), or higher-quality performance.

Once you get beyond budget camcorders, you should look for a model that includes a good-quality zoom lens, image stabilization (to keep your pictures steady, even if your hands aren't), a variety of automatic exposure modes, and some sort of built-in video editing. This last feature lets you perform in-camera edits between scenes, including audio dubbing, fade in and out, and other special effects.

The best camcorders today move beyond the traditional standard definition format to record movies in true high-definition video (HDV)—ideal for YouTube's high-definition playback. An HDV camcorder, like the one shown in Figure 13.4, offers all the features of a standard definition camcorder, but with the capability of recording high-definition signals onto a hard disk or memory card. And high-definition video is much better looking than standard definition video.

FIGURE 13.4   Sony's HDR-SR11 high-definition camcorder. (Photo courtesy Sony.)

Naturally, an HDV camcorder will shoot in the 16:9 aspect ratio, which is part of the high-definition format. You can also record Dolby Digital surround sound, although you'll probably need an external surround sound microphone for this.

There's one more thing you need to consider when choosing a camcorder, and that's the storage medium. Camcorders can store their video files on MiniDV videotapes, recordable DVD discs, built-in hard drives, or removable flash memory cards. Hard disk drive (HDD) and flash memory storage are best to work with for YouTube purposes, as you can quickly and easily transfer the video files from these media to your computer's hard disk. Some experts recommend flash memory as the best storage medium, period, as it doesn't add any moving parts to the camera—which improves reliability while reducing the overall weight. In any case, make sure you're comfortable with the way your camcorder stores video—and the way it transfers those files to your PC.

Shooting the Video

You can use your camcorder to shoot either indoors or outdoors. Shooting outdoors on a sunny day provides all the light you need for hiqh-quality pictures. Shooting indoors, however, might call for some additional equipment to bring the lighting up to acceptable standards. You should definitely consider mounting the camcorder on a sturdy tripod; additional lighting and an external microphone will help you achieve better results as well.

Start by placing the subject of your video in front of a plain, nondistracting background; if you can, choose a background color that contrasts with the subject's clothing or the color of the product being shot. Attach an external light on top of your camcorder, or set up two or more freestanding lights to the front and either side of the subject. And, for better sound, mic the subject with a lavaliere microphone—the kind you clip onto the subject's shirt or collar.

TIP: **Background Paper**
Consider investing in a roll or two of seamless photographic background paper and accompanying stands if it fits in your budget and you have space to store it. Also good are patterned muslin or cloth backdrops, all of which can be found at better photo retailers.

Once everything is set up (and take your time doing this; rushing things can create unsatisfactory results), run through the shoot a few times for practice. Once everyone is ready to go, shoot the video for real. If something goes wrong, stop the shoot and do another take. In fact, you should shoot several takes and use the best of the bunch in your final video.

You might also want to shoot the video again from another angle, or with close ups on the product or the demonstrator's hands or whatever aspect you might be emphasizing in the video. This gives you a library of shots you can use during the editing process; cutting away to a close up, for example, helps to increase the visual interest of the video. The key is to give yourself enough options to best edit the final video; don't paint yourself into a box with a single take of a static shot.

Tips for Shooting Better YouTube Videos

Some YouTube videos look better than others. That's because some users pay more attention to the details—which can greatly impact the results. With that in mind, here are a handful of tips that can help you avoid producing amateurish-looking videos.

Shoot Digitally

Not all YouTube videos are shot on new (or relatively new) digital camcorders. There are still quite a few older camcorders out there that record on analog cassettes. If you have one of these analog camcorders, throw it out and buy a new digital camcorder. You don't want to shoot on analog tape; the best results come from keeping an all-digital chain throughout the entire process.

Use a Tripod

One of the easiest ways to turn a good video into a mediocre one is to shoot it without a tripod. When you hold a camera in your hand, it *will* move; it's impossible for you to hold the camera perfectly still for the three minutes or so of the entire video. The result will be a jerky, jumpy picture that looks more like a home movie than it does a professional video production. That's not what you want.

Better results are obtained when you invest in a tripod. Mount the camera onto the tripod and it won't move around anymore. Your picture will stay stable and clear, with a much more professional look. It's the first and best investment you can make in your video production capabilities!

Lighting Matters

Shooting in available indoor light seldom achieves acceptable results. You can dramatically improve the look of your videos by adding more light—augmenting the available light with some sort of external light. This can be a camera-mounted video light, freestanding photofloods, or a full-blown video lighting kit. The key is to get more—and better—light into the shot.

TIP: **Buying Lights**

The best place to search for external lighting is at your local camera store. The same lighting kits that still photographers use work perfectly for video use.

The purpose of better lighting, by the way, isn't just to get rid of lingering shadows. Most indoor lighting isn't quite white; the color of white varies from light source to light source. Some types of lighting produce a cooler (bluer) white, while others produce a warmer (redder) white. And when the light itself is colored, it affects all the other colors in the shot. Studio lighting, on the other hand, is designed to have a more neutral cast—which is what you want for your videos.

Minimize the Background Noise—or Use an External Microphone

Most webcams and camcorders don't include high-quality microphones. This means that the sound you record is often of lower quality than might be desired. You can compensate by sitting as close to the camera as possible and speaking loudly and clearly. Don't mumble and don't whisper; enunciate as if you are speaking to an auditorium full of people.

You should also know that your webcam or camcorder will pick up any background noise in the room—which can be really distracting to YouTube viewers. So turn off any noisy mechanical or electronic devices, including fans, coffee machines, printers, you name it. And make sure that anyone else in the room with you stays quiet!

Even better, you might be able to attach an external microphone to your camcorder. (This isn't an option with webcams, unfortunately.) Many higher-end camcorders have an external microphone jack, to which you can connect most any type of external mic.

It's much better to use an external mic than an internal one; you can mic the subject directly rather than from across the room. The key is to get the mic closer to the subject and to isolate the subject from all other background sounds. You want to clearly hear what the subject is saying, and only what the subject is saying. The only way to do that is with an external microphone.

Watch the Background

Ever notice the background in a professionally shot video? Probably not—which speaks to the care in which it was chosen. You're not supposed to notice the background; your attention is supposed to be focused on the main subject.

The point here is that you need to pay particular attention to what's behind the subject in your shot. Don't point your camera at yourself sitting behind your desk without also examining what's behind you. If the background is too busy, it will distract from the subject; the viewer's eyes will drift to the background instead of to the person who's talking.

What kinds of backgrounds do you want to avoid? The list includes things like open windows (especially with people walking by outside!), busy wallpaper, cluttered bookshelves, and general clutter. It's much better to shoot in front of a plain wall, if you have no other choice.

Even better is to use some sort of professional background. Any good photography store sells seamless background paper, as well as cloth and muslin backgrounds with various unobtrusive patterns. If you do a lot of corporate videos, consider creating your own unique patterned background incorporating your company's logo, either large or in a smaller repeating pattern.

A Little Movement Is Good...

Not all YouTube videos need to be static. One of the advantages of using a camcorder is that, unlike a webcam, you can move a camcorder. So get your subject out of her chair and capture her walking across the room, or moving back and forth between a couple of props. Use the camera in a handheld fashion or, even better, put it on the tripod and turn the head of the tripod to follow the speaker's movement. Even in a small YouTube window, it's okay to have a little action in the shot.

...But Too Much Movement Is Bad

That said, a sure way to make your video look amateurish is to show off your camera technique by zooming in and out, panning back and forth, and otherwise moving your camera too much. While some camera movement is good, too much is bad. Don't overuse the zoom and pan; it just makes your video difficult to watch.

This is particularly so when your video is being shown in a small video window in a web browser, as it is with YouTube. On the web, extraneous motion is your enemy. Even well-crafted motion can sometimes detract from the message being delivered. When creating video for the web, you want to eliminate all unnecessary motion, both from the camera and from the subject.

Worse is high-motion action, such as when capturing sporting events. When each new frame of your video holds substantially different information from the previous frame, you end up unnecessarily increasing the size of your video file. In addition, someone viewing your video on a slow Internet connection might see the action as jerky and disconnected rather than smooth, which is not the effect you want.

For this reason, many video producers try to keep their subjects as stationary as possible in the frame. They also try to keep camera movement to a minimum—no unnecessary zooming, panning, or tilting when shooting a static shot will work just as well.

Shoot from Different Angles

Another way to introduce visual interest in your videos is to cut between multiple shots. You might show the presenter speaking directly to the camera, but then cut to a short shot of the presenter from the side. This sort of rapid cutting is simply more interesting than a static front-on shot held for three minutes.

You can accomplish this in a number of ways. The easiest way is to shoot the video twice—one from the first angle and one from a second angle. You can then intercut shots from both takes in the editing process.

Another approach is to shoot the video only once, but use two cameras, each placed at a different position. Again, you can intercut shots from both videos during the editing process. The advantage of this two-camera approach is that the two videos will be perfectly in sync, which is unlikely using a single-camera approach.

Close-Ups Are Good

While we're talking about using different shots in a video, consider the use of close-ups as one of your alternatives. Let's say you're shooting a how-to demonstration, which you shoot from an appropriate distance to capture both the presenter and the item. At some point, however, the presenter presses a particular button on the item, which is difficult to see from several feet away. The solution is to shoot a separate close-up shot of the presenter's finger on the button. You can then cut to this shot at the appropriate point in the video. This not only adds visual interest, it better demonstrates that facet of the item.

Don't Center the Subject

When shooting a video for YouTube, it's tempting to place your subject dead center in the video frame, as shown in Figure 13.5. Avoid the temptation—especially if you're shooting in widescreen.

FIGURE 13.5   Bad composition—positioning the subject dead center in the frame.

A much better compositional approach is to position the subject off-center, utilizing a technique called the *rule of thirds*. With the rule of thirds, you divide the frame into three vertical strips, as shown in Figure 13.6. Instead of placing the subject dead center in the middle segment, position the subject at or close to one of the two vertical grid lines. Whether it's left or right of center is entirely up to you.

> TIP: **Look Center**
>
> When you position your subject at one of the rule of third vertical lines, make sure you have him or her looking either directly into the camera or slightly into the center of the frame. The alternative is to have your subject staring out of the frame, which is a trifle disconcerting.

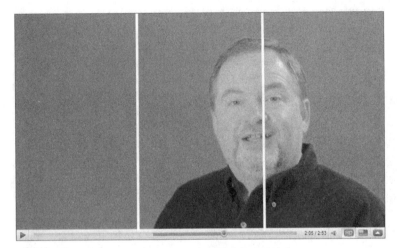

FIGURE 13.6   Better composition, using the rule of thirds.

Shoot to Edit

Editing is crucial to creating a professional-looking video. The best way to make your videos easier to edit is by shooting to edit—which means thinking about your final production before and during the shoot. This lets you capture appropriate shots during the process, as well as keep the shot somewhat efficient by shooting only what you need. Not only will you speed up the shooting process, you'll also be able to edit much faster when you get to that phase of the operation.

> NOTE: **Video Editing**
>
> You can edit together multiple takes, as well as insert transition effects and titles, using a video editing program. Learn more in Lesson 14, "Preparing a Video to Upload."

Keep It Short

YouTube lets you upload videos up to 10 minutes in length. When at all possible, your videos should come in shorter than this. People today—YouTube viewers in particular—have short attention spans, and you don't want viewers clicking away before your video is complete. For this reason, I recommend keeping your videos no more than two to three minutes long. In any case, the shorter the better.

Dress Appropriately

We'll finish our tips with a word about how the subject of your video should be dressed. The key word is "appropriately," as there's no single right or wrong dress code for every possible type of video.

The key thing is to consider how the chosen clothing will look onscreen. Avoid clothing with busy or small repeating patterns; plain shirts are better than striped ones. And don't let the color or brightness of the presenter's clothing conflict or blend in too much with the shot's background color or pattern. You want the subject to stand out from the background, but not glaringly so.

Summary

In this lesson, you learned how to shoot videos for YouTube. In the next lesson, you learn how to prepare your videos for uploading.

Preparing a Video to Upload

In this lesson, you learn how to edit your videos and convert them into the proper format for YouTube use.

Editing Your Videos

Few videos are YouTube-ready out of the box, not even those produced by professionals. You'll probably want to cut out the boring parts, trim the whole thing down to no more than 10 minutes (less is probably better), and convert the video to a YouTube-friendly MPEG-4 file. You might even want to add titles, onscreen graphics, scene transitions, and other special effects.

Sound like a lot of work? It doesn't have to be—assuming you have a well-powered personal computer and the right video-editing software.

Choosing a Video-Editing Program

In the not-so-distant past, if you wanted to edit a video, you had to use an expensive and dedicated video-editing console, like the ones found in local and network television studios. Not so today; any moderately powered personal computer, equipped with the right software, will do the job quite nicely—and at much lower cost. Today's video-editing software lets you cut and rearrange scenes, add fancy transitions between scenes, add titles (and subtitles), and even add your own music soundtrack. The results are amazing!

There are many different video-editing programs available. Some programs are free:

▶ Apple iMovie, part of the iLife software included free with all Macintosh computers

▶ Microsoft Windows Live Movie Maker, a free download from download.live.com

▶ Microsoft Windows Movie Maker, included free with Windows XP and Windows Vista

Other programs are what most of us would call "affordable"—less than $100. These programs include:

▶ Adobe Premiere Elements, $99.99 (www.adobe.com/products/premiereel/)

▶ ArcSoft ShowBiz DVD, $99.99 (www.arcsoft.com/en/products/showbiz/)

▶ CyberLink PowerDirector, $54.92 (www.cyberlink.com)

▶ MoviePlus, $79.99 (www.serif.com/movieplus/)

▶ Nero Ultra Edition, $99.99 (www.nero.com)

▶ Pinnacle Studio, $49.99 (www.pinnaclesys.com)

▶ Pinnacle Studio Plus, $79.99 (www.pinnaclesys.com)

▶ Roxio MyDVD Video Lab, $49.99 (www.roxio.com)

▶ Sony Vegas Movie Studio, $54.95 (www.sonycreativesoftware.com/products/vegasfamily.asp)

▶ Ulead VideoStudio X2, $99.99 (www.ulead.com/vs/)

NOTE: **Prices**

All prices listed here are current as of June, 2009, but are subject to change.

For most users, either the free or "affordable" programs will do just about everything you need to do. If you want more powerful editing and fancier special effects, however, you have to move up to the third tier of programs. These programs, priced from $200 to $500 or so, include the following:

▶ Apple Final Cut Express, $199 (Mac-only, www.apple.com/finalcutexpress/)

▶ Sony Vegas Pro, $599.95 (www.sonycreativesoftware.com/products/vegasfamily.asp)

▶ Ulead MediaStudio Pro, $399.99 (www.ulead.com/msp/)

Finally, if you want true professional-quality editing and effects—and money is no object—there are two more programs worth considering:

▶ Adobe Premiere Pro CS, $799 (www.adobe.com/products/premiere/)

▶ Apple Final Cut Studio, $1,299 (Mac-only, www.apple.com/finalcutstudio/)

Using a Video-Editing Program

Whether you use a free video-editing program or one that costs $1,000 or more, you use the program to do pretty much the same tasks—edit together multiple scenes, add titles and transitions before and between scenes, and apply any desired special effects. If the program allows, you can also choose to "clean up" your audio and video using various color correction and noise reduction tools.

How do you perform these essential tasks? Obviously, the specific steps vary from program to program, but the general approach remains the same.

Most of these programs let you piece together different files (often called *clips*) into a single video. You edit these clips together by arranging them on a type of timeline, like the one shown in Figure 14.1. You can then add transitions between clips, such as fades and wipes and such.

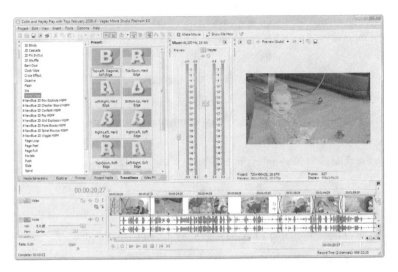

FIGURE 14.1   Use a video-editing program, such as Sony Vegas Movie Studio, to arrange multiple video clips into a single storyboard.

Just as important as scene transitions are the titles and credits you can add before and after the main body of your video. You can use a main title to introduce the video to YouTube viewers and you can use credits to provide more information at the end. You can even overlay graphics in the middle of the video—the better to grab the viewers' attention.

Many video-editing programs let you enhance your video with background music. You might even be able to add a variety of special video effects—such as decolorizing the video or making the video look like well-worn film stock. The more powerful (and expensive) the video-editing program, the more special effects available.

Finally, when you've done all your editing and applied all your transitions and special effects, it's time to save your work. In most video-editing programs, this is a two-step process: First you save the project and then you create the final video. This second step involves a lot of computer processing, as the video editing program compiles all the clips and effects you select into a single video file.

NOTE: **Creating the Video**

The process of creating a final video is sometimes called process-ing, publishing, or rendering the video.

Choosing a Computer for Video Editing

To run your video editing software, you need a fairly powerful computer. That's because video editing is the second-most demanding operation you can do on your PC. (The most demanding activity is playing games, believe it or not.) It takes a lot of processing power, memory, and hard disk storage to edit and process full-motion video, and most older and lower-priced PCs simply aren't up to the task. It might mean, depending on your unit, that you have some upgrading to do.

So, what kind of PC do you need for video editing? If you're an Apple user, there's no better computer for video editing than a Mac Pro. This machine has all the horsepower and all the features you need to do all sorts of fancy video editing without even breaking a sweat. If you're a Windows user, you have a lot more choices. To start with, you want to go with the fastest, most powerful processor you can afford. The best choices today are so-called quad-core machines, which run the equivalent of four processors in a single CPU. These are 64-bit processors, as opposed to the older 32-bit models, and run the 64-bit version of Windows.

Memory is an important part of the equation, too. The bare minimum required for video editing today is 4GB, although you should go for more memory if you can.

You'll also need lots of hard disk space, with a fast hard disk. Perhaps the best way to go is to add a dedicated external hard disk just for your video editing. Make sure the hard drive connects via FireWire because FireWire is faster for this type of data transfer than USB is.

When it comes to hard disk storage, bigger is better. For example, if you shoot a standard definition video at 5:1 compression, you'll need 3.6MB for every second of video you shoot. That's almost 13GB for a full hour of video. After you have a few videos (or even a few differently edited versions of the same video) on your hard disk, the space used starts getting big. For this reason, consider a big 1TB (terabyte) drive for your video storage. You can't have too much hard disk space.

TIP: **Hard Disk Space**

When calculating the necessary hard disc space, factor in the amount of "raw" video you have, not just the length of the final edited video. It's easy for your raw material to be ten times or more as long as your final product!

Obviously, your computer needs to have a USB connection, because that's how most digital camcorders connect. If you use a fast external hard drive that connects via FireWire (also called *iLink* or *IEEE 1394*), your PC needs a FireWire connection, as well.

Finally, consider what type of monitor you'll be using. Here again, bigger is better—at least 20" diagonal widescreen display. Although it might seem like overkill to use a big widescreen monitor to edit small-screen YouTube videos, all the components of your video-editing program take up a lot of screen space. In addition, you'll want to be able to display fully all your 720×1280 high-definition videos, which a larger display is much better suited to do.

Bottom line: If you're serious about video editing, especially in HD, you may need to invest in a new computer system. Fortunately, you can get a system that does all you need for less than $1,000 these days—considerably less, if you're a smart shopper.

Understanding Video File Formats

Before you create or render your first YouTube video, you need to know which file format to save it in. There are several different file formats used to store video information, each with its own advantages and limitations.

AVI

The Audio/Video Interleave format, commonly known as AVI, is an older Windows-only format. AVI is a container format, which means it can contain videos encoded in a number of different formats, combined with metadata about the video's contents.

PLAIN ENGLISH: **Container Format**
A file format that holds different types of data within the file. These formats, such as the AVI and RealVideo formats, contain not only the underlying audio and video, but also metadata about the source material—chapter information, subtitles, and such.

Digital Video (DV)

The Digital Video (DV) format is used in many digital camcorders, particularly those that use MiniDV cassettes. It's a lossy format, even though it doesn't create particularly small files.

DV-format video is typically enclosed in some type of container file format, such as AVI or QuickTime files. Because it encodes video at the full standard frame rate of 30 frames per second, videos encoded in the DV format can be edited on a frame-by-frame basis.

PLAIN ENGLISH: **Lossy Compression**
Video compression technology that results in some loss of quality in an attempt to reduce file sizes. Lossless compression results in no quality loss, but creates larger files.

Flash Video (FLV)

Flash video is the file format used by YouTube to deliver all its videos. The Flash video format (FLV extension) works with the Adobe Flash Player, on which the YouTube video player is based.

FLV files consist not only of the video file, but also a short header and other metadata. The video itself is encoded in an interleaved format.

H.264

The H.264 format is a subset of the MPEG-4 format. H.264, also known as Advanced Video Coding, is well-suited for dealing with high-definition video, such as HDTV broadcasts and Blu-ray discs. It encodes high-quality video at relatively low bit rates, which results in smaller file sizes— something that is particularly important, given the huge native file sizes of high-definition video.

The H.264 format is used for all YouTube videos, as well as all videos available on Apple's iTunes Store.

MPEG

Perhaps the most popular video file format today is the MPEG format— or, to be precise, one of several MPEG formats—MPEG-1, MPEG-2, and MPEG-4. Each format offers progressively better audio/video quality at progressively higher compression rates—which results in better picture and sound in smaller file sizes.

> PLAIN ENGLISH: **MPEG**
>
> Moving Pictures Expert Group, a committee that sets international standards for the digital encoding of audio and video.

Here's how each of the MPEG formats compare:

- ▶ **MPEG-1**. This is the original MPEG format, used originally in the now-extinct Video CD (VCD) format. It's still used in some digital camcorders, as it creates small, easily transferrable video formats; the video quality, however, is only about VHS level. Because of the resulting small file sizes, MPEG-1 remains somewhat popular for posting clips on the Internet.

- ▶ **MPEG-2.** This later version of the MPEG standard produces much higher quality audio and video than the original MPEG-1

format while still maintaining small(ish) file sizes. It's commonly used in commercial DVDs, digital satellite broadcasts, TiVo
and other brands of digital video recorders, and some broadcast
television applications. Picture quality is close to the DV format.

▶ **MPEG-4.** This is the latest iteration of the MPEG standard,
designed with both the Internet and high-definition video in
mind. It uses improved coding efficiency to produce higher-quality video in smaller-sized files; it's used in many newer digital
camcorders, some digital satellite systems, broadcast HDTV, and
streaming Internet videos.

> NOTE: **MPEG-3**
>
> Wondering about the missing MPEG-3 format? It was initially devel-
> oped for high-definition video, but it was abandoned when experts
> realized that MPEG-2 could be extended for that purpose.

QuickTime Movie (MOV)

The QuickTime Movie (MOV) format is Apple's proprietary video format, used in Apple's QuickTime media player. It works on both the Mac
OS and Windows.

Windows Media Video (WMV)

The Windows Media Video (WMV) format is Microsoft's proprietary
video format, playable with Microsoft's Windows Media Player.
Microsoft claims that the bitrate is twice that of MPEG-4; the result is
better video quality, but with larger-sized files.

Configuring Your Videos to Upload

Now that you're familiar with the various video file formats, which format
should you use to upload your videos to YouTube? You have several
choices.

Choosing the File Format

For what it's worth, YouTube stores and serves its videos in Flash video (FLV) format, using H.264 compression. You can upload your videos to YouTube in your choice of the AVI, Flash (FLV), MPEG-4 (MPG), QuickTime (MOV), or Windows Media Video (WMV) file formats. You can also upload from your cell phone in either 3GP or MP4 formats. Once your files are uploaded, YouTube automatically converts your videos to FLV files.

Choosing the Resolution

File format isn't the only important technical issue to keep in mind. Resolution and frame rate also affect the ultimate quality of your videos when they're played on YouTube. Here's what you need to know:

▶ If you've shot your video in standard resolution at the traditional 4:3 aspect ratio, you should render your files at 640 × 480 resolution—what YouTube calls "high-quality."

▶ If you've shot your video in standard resolution but at the widescreen 16:9 aspect ratio, you should render your files at 720 × 480 resolution.

▶ If you've shot your video with a high-definition camcorder, you should render your files at 1280 × 720 resolution—to match YouTube's high-definition format.

Other Settings

There are a few other settings you need to keep in mind when rendering your videos:

▶ **Length**: YouTube accepts videos up to 10 minutes in length. Anything longer should be broken down into multiple files.

▶ **File size**. Length aside, the files you upload can be no more than 100MB in size. When you're uploading a high-definition video, you'll probably hit the file size constraint before you hit the 10-minute limit.

▶ **Audio**. Most video editing programs handle audio conversion automatically, but if you have a choice, go with MP3 format audio.

▶ **Frame rate**. The best choice is to go with the native frame rate—that is, the frame rate shot by your camera. While not all cameras or video editing programs offer this optoin, when you can choose, go with a 30 frames per second (FPS) rate.

Summary

In this lesson, you learned how to edit and prepare your videos for uploading. In the next lesson, you learn how to upload these videos to the YouTube site.

Uploading a Video to YouTube

In this lesson, you learn how to upload videos to the YouTube site.

Uploading a Video from Your PC

Most videos you create with a camcorder or webcam are saved as files on your computer's hard drive. This video file is what you upload to YouTube.

To upload a video file, it must be in a YouTube-approved format, be less than 10 minutes long, and be smaller than 100MB. If your video meets these requirements, you're ready to upload.

> NOTE: **Video Formats**
> Learn more about YouTube-approved video formats in Lesson 14, "Preparing a Video to Upload."

To upload a video, follow these steps:

1. Click the Upload button at the top of any YouTube page, then select Upload Video File.

2. When the Video File Upload page appears, click the Upload Video button.

3. When the next dialog box appears, navigate to and select the file to upload, then click the Open button.

4. While the video uploads, you're prompted to enter information about the video, as shown in Figure 15.1. Start by entering a title for your video into the Title box.

5. Enter a brief description of your video into the Description box.

6. Enter one or more tags for the video into the Tags box, separating each tag by a space.

PLAIN ENGLISH: **Tag**

A keyword that viewers enter when searching the YouTube site. The tags you enter for your video should be those keywords that viewers might enter if they're looking for videos like yours.

---

7. Pull down the Category list and select the best category for your video.

8. If you want all YouTube users to be able to view your video, check the Share Your Video with the World option. If you prefer to keep your video private, check the Private option.

9. Click the Save Changes button.

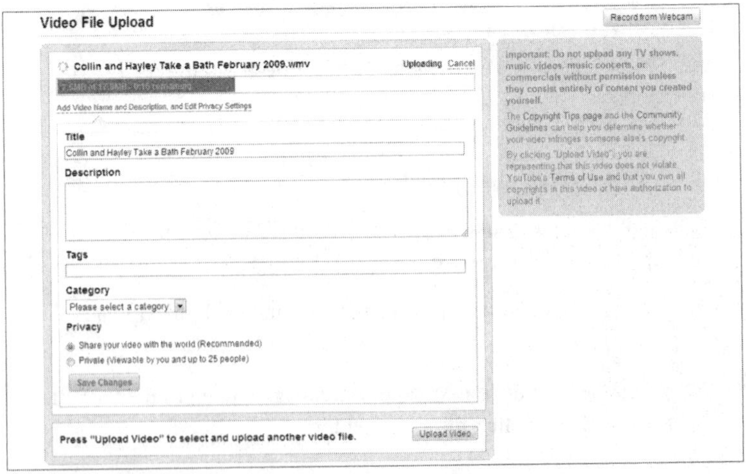

FIGURE 15.1   Entering information about an uploaded video.

That's it. After the video uploads, YouTube converts it to the proper viewing format and creates a viewing page for the video. To view your video, click the My Videos link on any YouTube page and then click the thumbnail for your new video.

Uploading a Video from Your Webcam Using Quick Capture

If you have a webcam connected to your PC, you have two ways of uploading webcam videos to YouTube:

▶ You can save your webcam videos as you do normally and then upload those videos via YouTube's normal video upload process.

▶ You can upload videos as you shoot them, "live" from your webcam, using YouTube's Quick Capture feature.

CAUTION: **No Editing**

When you use Quick Capture to upload "live" webcam videos to YouTube, you don't have the opportunity to edit those videos; whatever you record is what gets shown on YouTube, warts and all.

To record and upload a webcam session using Quick Capture, follow these steps:

1. With your webcam connected and running, click the Upload button on any YouTube page then select Record from Webcam. This displays the Quick Capture page, shown in Figure 15.2.

2. You should now see the picture from your webcam in the video window; click the Ready to Record button to start recording.

CAUTION: **Allow Recording**

If you see a message that says YouTube is requesting access to your camera and microphone, click the Allow button, then click Close.

---

3. When you're finished with the recording, click the red Record button.

4. If you don't like what you recorded, click the Re-Record button to make a new recording.

5. If you're happy with what you recorded, click the Publish button. YouTube now uploads the video to the site and converts it into the appropriate playback format, then displays a new Video Details page for this video.

6. Fill in the appropriate blanks on the Video Details page and click the Save Changes button.

FIGURE 15.2   Getting ready to record a "live" webcam video with Quick Capture.

Uploading Videos from Your Mobile Phone

Finally, if your mobile phone has a built-in video camera, you can upload videos directly from your cell phone without first copying them to your PC. All you have to do is set up YouTube's mobile upload options and then email your videos to the YouTube site.

To configure YouTube for your mobile phone, click the Account link at
the top of any YouTube page. When your Account page appears, click the
Mobile Setup link on the left side of the page. YouTube now generates a
unique email address to use when uploading videos from your mobile
phone, typically in the form of *username+numbers*@m.youtube.com.

To upload a video from your mobile phone, simply email the video from
your phone to this address. You'll be notified via email or text message
when YouTube has received the email and begun processing the video;
you can then go to YouTube's website and edit specific information about
the newly uploaded video.

Summary

In this lesson, you learned three different ways to upload videos to
YouTube. In the next lesson, you learn how to edit the information you
provide about your videos.

LESSON 16

Editing Video Information

In this lesson, you learn how to edit the information you provide about your videos.

Editing Information

After you've uploaded a video to YouTube, you can edit any and all information you provided about that video. Follow these steps:

1. Click the down arrow next to your username at the top of any YouTube page, then click My Videos.

   You now see the Uploaded Videos page, shown in Figure 16.1, which displays all the videos you've uploaded to YouTube.

2. Click the Edit button next to the video you want to edit.

3. When the Info & Settings page for that video appears, as shown in Figure 16.2, edit any of the information boxes as necessary.

4. Click the Save Changes button when done.

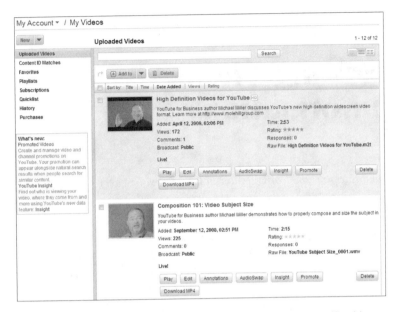

FIGURE 16.1 Click the Edit button to edit information for a specific video.

FIGURE 16.2 Editing information about your video.

You can edit the following information about your video:

► Title

► Description

► Tags

► Category

► Video thumbnail

► Privacy—Share or Private

► Friends allowed to view Private videos

► Comments—allow all comments automatically, allow friends' comments automatically/approve other comments, allow comments with approval only, don't allow comments

---

TIP: **Comments**

If you don't want to display negative comments about your video, you can either disable comments or opt to approve all comments before they're posted. (The same goes with video responses, comment voting, and ratings.)

► Comment voting—allow or not

► Video responses—allow automatically, allow with approval only, don't allow

► Ratings—allow or not

► Embedding—allow or not

TIP: **Embedding**

If you don't want your video shown on other websites, opt to not allow embedding.

► Syndication (viewing on mobile phones and TV)—allow or not

▶ Date and map—provide date and location details for geomapping of the video

> PLAIN ENGLISH: **Geomapping**
> Embeds location information into a YouTube video, so that video can be associated with (and searched by) a specific location.

Changing the Video Thumbnail

Don't like the image that YouTube automatically displays for a video? As noted in the previous section, YouTube lets you select the thumbnail image that is displayed for your video on search pages, browse pages, and the like.

To change the thumbnail for your video, go to the Uploaded Videos page and click the Edit button for that video. Scroll to the Video Thumbnail section, shown in Figure 16.3, and you see three frames that YouTube has pulled from your video. Click the image you want to use for your video's thumbnail.

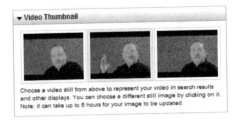

FIGURE 16.3   Changing your video's thumbnail image.

Removing a Video from YouTube

When a video is no longer relevant, its page views have dropped off, or if you decide you just don't like it, you can remove any one of your videos from the YouTube site; otherwise, it will stay online forever.

To remove a video from YouTube, follow these steps:

1. Click the down arrow next to your username at the top of any YouTube page, then click My Videos.

2. When the Uploaded Videos page appears, check those videos you want to delete.

3. Click the Delete button at the top of the Uploaded Videos page.

CAUTION: **Think Twice**

Think twice before you click the Delete button. All videos you remove are permanently deleted from the YouTube site; you'll need to re-upload the video if you click the Delete button by mistake.

Summary

In this lesson, you learned how to edit and delete videos you've uploaded to YouTube. In the next lesson, you learn how to replace the original audio on a video with a new soundtrack.

LESSON 17

Swapping Audio on a Video

In this lesson, you learn how to replace a video's audio track with a new soundtrack.

Why Swap Audio?

Some YouTube users upload videos that are montages of either video clips or pictures in a slideshow. For these types of video, the best audio is a musical soundtrack.

Unfortunately, not all users have the skills or video-editing software necessary to add this type of musical soundtrack to their videos. It's also possible that you've already created such a soundtrack, but you're using commercial music for which you don't own the copyright.

For these situations, YouTube makes it easy to replace the existing sound on a video with a fully licensed musical soundtrack. Essentially, you delete the original audio and replace it with a song selected from YouTube's licensed music library. It's easy to do and completely legal; you don't have to worry about using the wrong music and having your video removed by YouTube.

CAUTION: **Copyrighted Music**

Most music on commercial CDs from your favorite recording artists is copyrighted. You cannot use this music without permission from the copyright holder. If you upload a video to YouTube that uses unauthorized music—even if it's just playing in the background of a home movie—the copyright holder can (and probably will) ask YouTube to remove the video.

Using AudioSwap

You can use YouTube's AudioSwap feature to replace your video's existing audio track with a new musical soundtrack. Here's how it works:

1. Click the down arrow next to your username at the top of any YouTube page, then click My Videos.

2. When the Uploaded Videos page appears, click the AudioSwap button next to the video you want to edit, as shown in Figure 17.1.

FIGURE 17.1   Click the AudioSwap button on the Uploaded Videos page.

3. You now see the AudioSwap page, shown in Figure 17.2. To display those songs that best match the length of your video, check the Only Show Songs of Similar Length to My Video option.

4. If you want YouTube to choose a song for your video at random, click the I'm Feeling Lucky button.

5. To search for songs that have something in common with your video, enter one or more keywords or tags that describe your video into the Or Browse Our Audio Track Library box, and then press Enter. This will display a list of songs that contains those keywords.

6. To browse through the available songs in YouTube's music library, select a Genre and/or Artist from the list.

7. Click the song you want to use for your video.

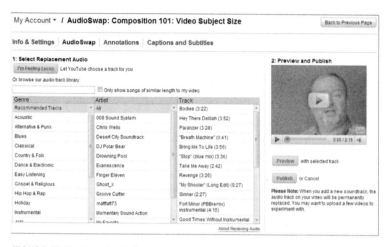

FIGURE 17.2 Use AudioSwap to replace your existing audio with a new song.

8. Click the Preview button to hear how your video sounds with the new soundtrack.

9. Click the Publish button to replace your original soundtrack with the selected song.

CAUTION: **Audio Replacement**
When you click the Publish button on the AudioSwap page, the existing audio for your video is fully deleted. If you want to restore the original audio, you have to re-upload the video.

Summary

In this lesson, you learned how to replace the audio in a YouTube video. In the next lesson, you learn how to add closed captions to your videos.

Adding Closed Captioning to Your Video

In this lesson, you learn how to add closed captions and subtitles to a YouTube video.

Why Add Closed Captioning or Subtitles?

When a video employs closed captioning technology, captions appear onscreen that describe what the audio is saying. It's a great boon to the hard of hearing; being able to read what others can hear makes the world of video programming more useful. For that matter, closed captioning is also useful if you want to listen to your videos with the sound turned down or muted—which you might do at work or after your kids have gone to bed.

PLAIN ENGLISH: **Closed Captioning**
The dialog of a video in written text format, typically used by deaf viewers to read what is being said in the video.

In addition, closed captioning technology can be used to add subtitles in an alternate language. For example, if a video has Japanese dialog, you could add English subtitles so that American viewers could understand it. Vice versa if you want to present an English-language video to a foreign audience.

Finally, closed captioning provides a text transcript of your entire video. This is useful for anyone who wants to examine the content of your video in more detail. It also helps people search for your video, as the transcript file itself can be searched by Google and other search engines.

Adding Closed Captions

To add closed captions or subtitles to a YouTube video, you must first create a closed caption file. This file contains the dialog for your video in a special format readable by closed caption players.

NOTE: **Closed Caption Formats**

YouTube supports closed caption files in the SubViewer (.SUB) and SubRip (.SRT) formats.

You create a closed caption file using special closed caption software or websites. The most popular closed caption software programs are MovCaptioner (www.synchrimedia.com) and Subtitle Workshop (www.urusoft.net). The most popular closed caption websites are CaptionTube (captiontube.appspot.com) and Easy YouTube Caption Creator (www.accessify.com/tools-and-wizards/accessibility-tools/easy-youtube-caption-creator/). Both let you create closed caption files online from any web browser.

Once you've created a closed caption or subtitle file using one of these tools, you can add it to your YouTube video by following these steps:

1. Click the down arrow next to your username at the top of any YouTube page, then click My Videos.

2. When the Uploaded Videos page appears, click the Edit button next to the video to which you want to add closed captioning.

3. When the next page appears, click the Captions and Subtitles link in the menu bar.

4. When the Captions and Subtitles page appears, as shown in Figure 18.1, click the Choose a File button.

FIGURE 18.1   Adding closed captions to a video.

5. When the Open dialog box appears, navigate to and select the closed caption file, then click the Open button. The Closed Captions box now expands, as shown in Figure 18.2.

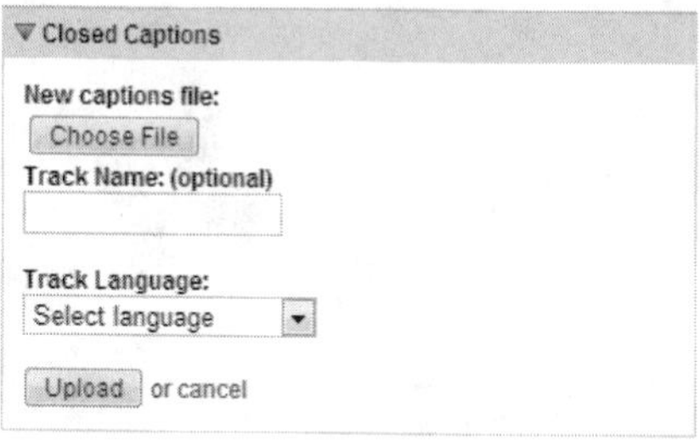

FIGURE 18.2   Enter a name and language for the closed captioning.

6. Enter a name for the closed caption or subtitle track into the Track Name box.

7. Pull down the Track Language list and select the language for the track. (This is important if you're adding subtitles in a different language.)

8. Click the Upload button.

> TIP: **Multiple Subtitles**
> If you want to add multiple subtitles in different languages, simply upload a separate file for each language.

Playing a Video with Closed Captions

Once closed captioning or subtitles have been added to a video, you can view the closed captions by clicking the up arrow at the bottom right of the video player window and selecting Turn on Captions (the CC button). The captions or subtitles now appear at the bottom of the video itself, as shown in Figure 18.3.

FIGURE 18.3   A video with closed captions.

Summary

In this lesson, you learned how to add closed captions and subtitles to a video. In the next lesson, you learn how to annotate your YouTube videos.

Adding Annotations to Your Video

In this lesson, you learn how to annotate your videos with note boxes, speech bubbles, and the like.

Understanding Annotations

Want to make your video a bit more interactive? Then consider adding annotations to your videos, so that viewers can click on the video to view additional information, links to other videos, and the like.

A YouTube annotation is like an overlay put on top of a normal video. The overlay can be a speech bubble, such as those used on pop-up video programs, or a note containing a link to another YouTube video or user channel. Viewers see your annotations when they click a specific area on the video screen. These overlays can also be used to pause the video playback.

You can add annotations to any video you've uploaded. You specify where the annotation appears in the video playback, what area of the screen is clickable, and what happens when that area is clicked.

YouTube lets you add three types of annotations, all shown in Figure 19.1:

▶ Speech bubble

▶ Note, which is a simple text box

▶ Spotlight, which appears only when the user moves his mouse over the overlay area

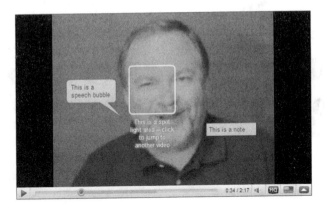

FIGURE 19.1   A video annotated with a pop-up speech bubble, a note, and a spotlight area.

TIP: **Pause Annotations**
You can also add a Pause annotation that pauses your video when the viewer clicks it. There is no text association with this type of annotation.

All three types of annotations can include both text and clickable links. You can link your annotations to other YouTube videos, playlists, channels, groups, and search queries.

NOTE: **Automatic Display**
Unlike spotlights, both speech bubbles and notes appear automatically at the selected point in the video. No involvement from the viewer is needed.

The overlay for the annotation can be any size and placed anywhere on the video window. You can place multiple annotations on screen at the same time or you can use them at different times throughout the video.

> CAUTION: **No Outside Links**
> You can link only to pages (videos, channels, groups, etc.) on the YouTube site. You can't link to non-YouTube web pages.

Annotating a Video

To add annotations to an existing YouTube video, follow these steps:

1. Click the down arrow next to your user name at the top of any YouTube page, then click My Videos.

2. When the Uploaded videos page appears, click the Annotations button next to the video you want to annotate. This displays the Annotations page for that video, as shown in Figure 19.2.

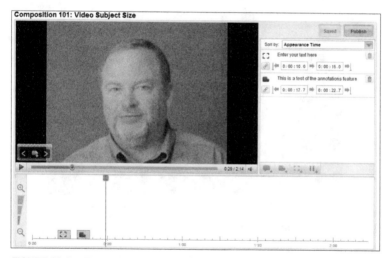

FIGURE 19.2 The Annotations page for a YouTube video.

3. Play or fast forward the video to the point where you want the annotation to begin.

4. Click the Add Annotation (+) button at the lower-left corner of the video, as shown in Figure 19.3, and select the type of annotation you want to add: Speech Bubble, Note, Spotlight, or Pause.

FIGURE 19.3   Select the type of annotation to add.

5. The overlay for the annotation now appears onscreen, as shown in Figure 19.4. Use your mouse to drag the overlay into the desired position or to resize the overlay as necessary.

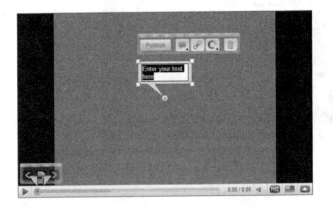

FIGURE 19.4   Creating a video annotation.

6. Enter the desired text into the annotation's text box.

7. If you want the annotation to include a clickable link, click the Add Annotation Link button to display the Add Link box; pull down the Link Type list and select the type of link; enter the URL for the link into the link box; and then click the Save button.

8. To change the color of the annotation, click the Change
    Annotation Color button.

9. Drag the right and left positioning cursors (located above the
    video's playback slider) to establish the start and stop points for
    this annotation.

10. Click the Publish button to save the annotation to your video.

Watching an Annotated Video

Watching an annotated video is like watching any YouTube video. At a
given point in the video, the annotations will appear onscreen. Spotlight
annotations, of course, are visible only when you hover your cursor over
that area of the screen. If an annotation contains a link, you can click that
link to go to the given video, channel, or group.

If you prefer not to see annotations for a video, click the up arrow at the
bottom-right corner of the video and select Turn Off Annotations, as
shown in Figure 19.5. To turn annotations back on, click the up arrow
again and select Turn On Annotations.

FIGURE 19.5 Turning off annotations for a video.

Summary

In this lesson, you learned how to add annotations to your YouTube videos. In the next lesson, you learn how to manage all the videos you upload.

LESSON 20

Managing Viewer Comments

In this lesson, you learn how to deal with user comments and video responses to your videos.

Enabling or Disabling Comments and Video Responses

One of the fun things about uploading videos to YouTube is that you get to see the comments and responses from people who've viewed your videos. Although it can be fun, it isn't always pleasant—which is why YouTube lets you manage these comments.

At your discretion, you can allow, disallow, or allow with prior approval either comments or video responses for any individual video you upload. This means you can allow comments for one video while disallowing comments for another.

> PLAIN ENGLISH: **Video Response**
> A video uploaded by another viewer in response to your video.

To control comments and video responses, follow these steps:

1. Click the down arrow next to your username at the top of any YouTube page, then click My Videos.

2. When the Uploaded Videos page appears, click the Edit button next to the video you want to edit.

3. When the Info & Settings page for that video appears, scroll to the Broadcasting and Sharing Options section, shown in Figure 20.1.

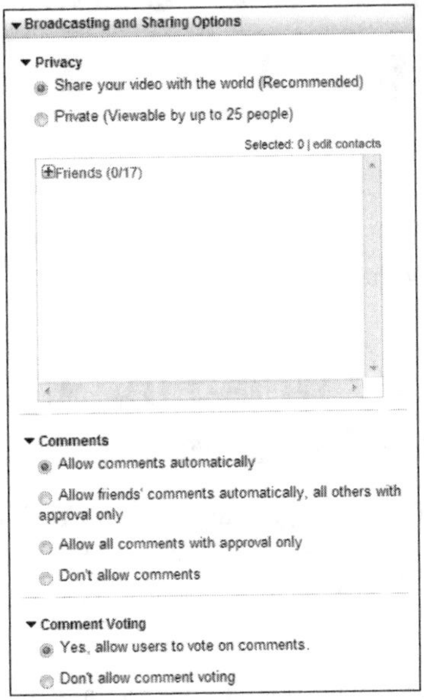

FIGURE 20.1   Changing comment behavior for a video.

4. To change comment behavior, select any of the following from the Comments section: Allow Comments Automatically (default); Allow Friends' Comments Automatically, All Others with Approval Only; Allow All Comments with Approval Only; or Don't Allow Comments.

5. To allow or disallow comment voting, go to the Comment Voting section and select either Yes (default), Allow Users to Vote on Comments, or Don't Allow Comment Voting.

TIP: **Expand the Section**
If a given section on the Info & Settings page isn't visible, click the title of that section to expand it to view all available options.

6. To change video response behavior, go to the Video Responses section and select one of the following: Yes, Allow Video Responses to Be Added Automatically; Yes, Allow Responses After I Approve Them; or No, Don't Allow Video Responses.

7. To enable or disable your video to be rated, go to the Ratings section and select either Yes, Allow This Video to Be Rated by Others or No, Don't Allow This Video to Be Rated.

8. Click the Save Changes button.

In general, your options fall along these lines:

▶ To allow comments and responses of all types with no intervention on your part, select the "allow all comments automatically" option.

▶ To personally approve all comments and responses before they're posted, select the "allow comments after I approve them" option.

▶ To not allow any comments or responses, select the "don't allow comments" option.

Approving Comments and Video Responses

If you choose the "with approval" option for comments or video responses, you have to manually approve any comments or responses viewers post to this video. When a viewer posts a comment or response, YouTube sends you an email. When you receive this email, go to the YouTube site and click the email link at the top of any YouTube page, and then click the Comments (for text comments) or Video Responses (for video responses) link on the left side of the page.

This displays a list of all pending comments/responses in your inbox, as shown in Figure 20.2. Click the message link to display the specific comment. From here you can choose to Approve or Ignore the pending comments.

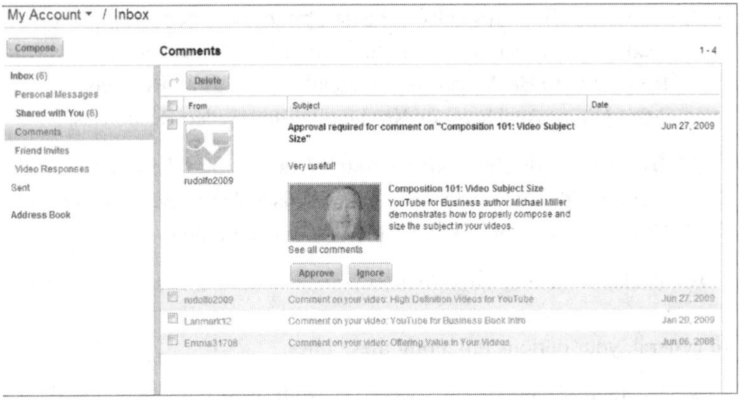

FIGURE 20.2 Approving viewer comments.

Removing Viewer Comments and Responses

What happens if someone posts a comment or video response that you find offensive—or just don't like? Fortunately, YouTube lets you remove individual comments and responses, even if you've configured that video's settings to automatically allow all comments and responses.

All you have to do is go to the page for that specific video and find the comment or response you want to remove. Click the Remove link beside that comment or response, as shown in Figure 20.3, and it is deleted.

FIGURE 20.3 Removing an unwanted comment by clicking the Remove link.

Blocking Members from Leaving Comments

Every now and then you'll run into a virtual stalker—some disgruntled type who delights in leaving negative comments on all your videos. While you can manually remove all of this user's comments, a better approach is to keep him from leaving those comments in the first place.

To this end, YouTube lets you block members from leaving comments and responses (and from sending personal messages to your YouTube inbox). To block a user, follow these steps:

1. Click the offending user's name.

2. When the user's channel page appears, scroll to the user information box, shown in Figure 20.4.

3. Click the Block User link.

FIGURE 20.4   Blocking a user.

This user will now be blocked from commenting on your videos and contacting you.

TIP: **Blocking from Comments**

If a user has commented on one of your videos, you can block that user directly from the video page. Just click the Block User link beside that user's comments.

Summary

In this lesson, you learned how to manage comments and responses to your videos. In the next lesson, you learn how to customize your YouTube channel page.

LESSON 21

Customizing Your YouTube Channel

In this lesson, you learn how to personalize your YouTube channel page.

Understanding Channels

Every user on YouTube has his or her own *channel*. On YouTube, a channel is just a fancy name for a user's profile; as soon as you post your first video, you create your own YouTube channel. At that point, other users can access your channel to see all the videos you've uploaded; users can also subscribe to your channel to be notified when you upload new videos to the YouTube site.

YouTube viewers access your channel page to learn more about you—and to look at all the videos you've uploaded. A viewer accesses your channel by clicking on your user name wherever it appears on the YouTube site. Although each profile page is unique, all pages contain the same major elements, as shown in Figure 21.1:

- ▶ Information about the user, including a link to subscribe to this channel

- ▶ Videos uploaded by this user

- ▶ Links to contact the user via email, leave comments, and access the user's non-YouTube website

- ▶ Links to the user's favorite videos, playlists, groups, friends, and the like

- ▶ The user's recent activity—videos uploaded, recent favorites, recent subscriptions, and the like

- ▶ Subscribers to the user's channel
- ▶ Comments on this user's channel
- ▶ The user's favorite videos
- ▶ Channels the user is watching

FIGURE 21.1   A typical YouTube channel page.

If a viewer likes what he sees on your channel page, he can subscribe to it. When a viewer subscribes to your channel, he is automatically notified (via email) when you upload new videos.

> NOTE: **Subscribing**
> Learn more about subscriptions in Lesson 7, "Subscribing to Videos."

Personalizing Your Channel Page

Because a YouTube channel page is really a profile page, you'll want to customize the look of your page to reflect your own personal style and tastes. It's easy to do.

You personalize your channel page from your My Account page. Follow these steps:

1. Click the Account link at the top of any YouTube page.

2. When the My Account page appears, click the Edit Channel link in the More section, shown in Figure 21.2.

3. When the Edit Channel Info page appears, click the Channel Design link on the left side of the page.

4. This displays your current channel page but with editing buttons along the top, as shown in Figure 21.3. Click each button to edit specific things about your channel page: Settings, Themes and Colors, and Modules.

My Videos	My Network	More
Uploaded Videos	Inbox	Groups
Favorites	Address Book	Active Sharing
Playlists	Subscribers	Edit Channel
Subscriptions	Video Comments	Custom Video Players
QuickList	Video Responses	Change Password
History		
Purchases		

FIGURE 21.2   Getting ready to edit your channel, from the My Account page.

FIGURE 21.3   Click a button to edit parts of your channel page.

Editing Channel Settings

When you click the Settings button, you see a new Settings panel at the top of your Channel page, as shown in Figure 21.4. This panel lets you edit your channel page's title and the tags you assign to your channel. Make the appropriate changes and click the Save Changes button when you're done.

FIGURE 21.4   Editing the title and tags for a channel.

Editing Channel Themes and Colors

When you want to change the look and feel of your channel page, click the Themes and Colors button. This expands the top of the channel page to display the Themes and Colors pane, shown in Figure 21.5. Click a color theme to switch your channel to that theme.

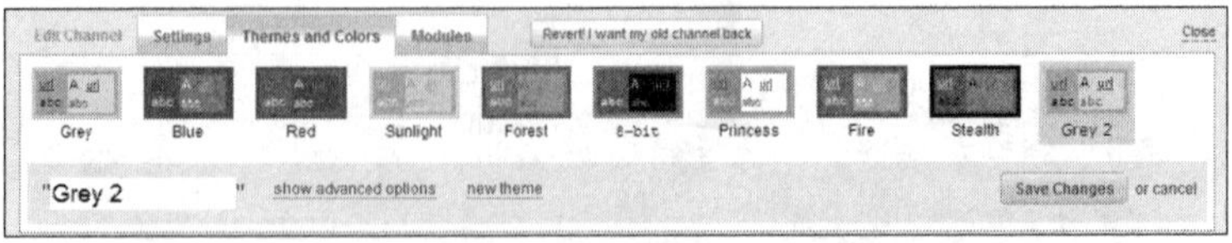

FIGURE 21.5   Changing your channel's color scheme.

If you want even more personalization, click the Show Advanced Options link. This expands the Themes and Colors pane even further, with options to control the color of various page elements. This expanded pane also enables you to add your own background image to your channel page; click the Choose File button in the Background Image section to select a JPEG or GIF image for the background. You can opt to display the image once on your page (default) or repeat the image through a longer page (check the Repeat Background option).

When you're done making changes, click the Save Changes button.

Editing Channel Modules

You can also control what content displays on your channel page. Click the Modules button to display the Modules pane, shown in Figure 21.6. You can choose to display any or all of the following content modules:

▶ Comments

▶ Subscribers

▶ Friends

▶ Subscriptions

▶ Recent activity

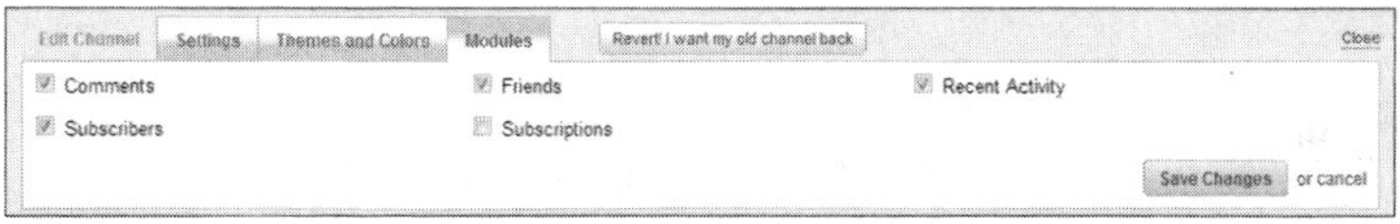

FIGURE 21.6   Selecting the content modules for your channel page.

Click the Save Changes button when done.

> NOTE: **Default Content**
>
> Your custom content modules supplement the default content displayed on all channel pages: user information, Uploads, Favorites, and a big featured video.

Summary

In this lesson, you learned how to customize your channel page. In the next lesson, you learn how to track the viewership of your videos.

LESSON 22

Tracking Viewership

In this lesson, you learn how to gather information about who is watching your videos.

Tracking Basic Viewership

Curious about how popular your videos are? Want to know more about who is watching your video? Fortunately, YouTube provides a number of metrics you can use to track the performance of each video you post.

YouTube's first tool for tracking the performance of a video is located right on the page for each video, on the Statistics & Data tab that's just below the video player. When you click this tab, you see a variety of statistics, as shown in Figure 22.1. These statistics include:

▶ Honors for this video—any awards the video has garnered

▶ Favorited—the number of users who have added this video to their favorites list

▶ Sites linking to this video—other websites that link back to the video

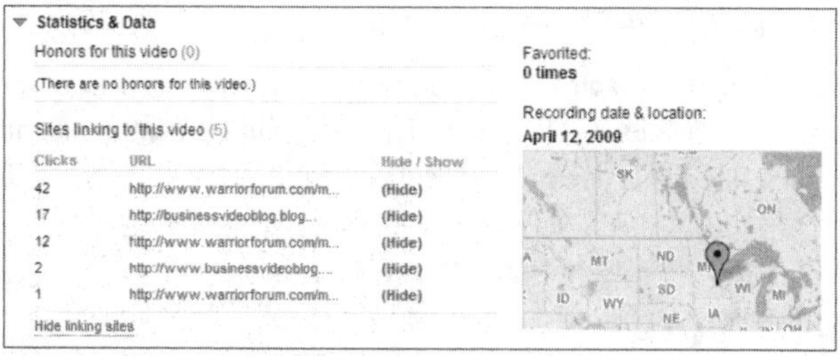

FIGURE 22.1 Tracking viewership on the Statistics & Data tab of a video page.

Also useful is the Views statistic, located directly under the video player window. This tells you the total number of times the video has been viewed.

TIP: **Clicks**
The list of sites that link back to the video includes a count of the actual clicks that have been made from that site to your video on the YouTube site.

Of course, the Views statistics makes one wonder how many views is a good number. That's hard to say. Certainly, if your video gets a million views overnight, you're doing something right—that's pure viral status. But, for certain types of videos, a total of 100 views might be good. You have to judge performance based on your own parameters and have realistic expectations.

Tracking Advanced Statistics

If you want more detailed information about the performance of a video, turn to YouTube's Insight tool. Insight lets you drill down through the data to view activity by geographic region over selected time periods. You can even see how your video compares to other videos uploaded from particular geographic regions.

To access the Insight tool, click the down arrow next to your username at the top of any YouTube page, then click My Videos. Next to each video on the My Videos page is an Insight button; click this button to display the Insight page for that video.

The Insight page for each video includes five tabs, selected from the left side of the page—Views, Discovery, Demographics, Community, and Hot Spots. Each tab displays a particular type of information, as we'll discuss next.

Insight Views

The Insight Views tab, shown in Figure 22.2, presents a graphical display of the number of views for your video, both over time and by region.

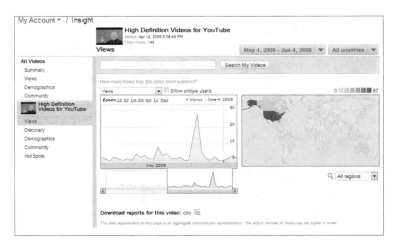

FIGURE 22.2 Using the Insight Views tab to analyze the viewcount for a video by time and region.

The left graph displays the number of views over the designated time period. You can expand or contract the graph to show views for the past 1 day, 5 days, 1 month, 3 months, 6 months, 1 year, or total video life (Max). Once you choose a length, you can use the slider beneath the graph to show performance for other time periods over the life of the video.

> **NOTE: All Views**
> YouTube's viewcount data includes views of the video on the YouTube site as well as views from other sites on which the video is embedded.

The right image is a map of the world with the number of views for your video displayed in different colors for each region. To select a specific country, click that country on the map; to select a larger region, select that region from the pull-down list beneath the graph.

> NOTE: **Regions**
>
> Insight analyzes performance for the following regions: USA, Asia, Africa, Europe, Middle East, and South America.

When you select a country or region, the viewcount for that area appears in the left graph. You can return that graph to a worldview by clicking the Back to All Countries link.

Insight Discovery

The Insight Discovery tab, shown in Figure 22.3, tells you how viewers discovered your video. The table on this page displays the top sources where your video was discovered. These methods include the following:

▶ YouTube Search

▶ Embedded Player (your video embedded on other sites)

▶ YouTube Other

▶ External Links

▶ Google Search

▶ Google Video

▶ Viral/Other [?]

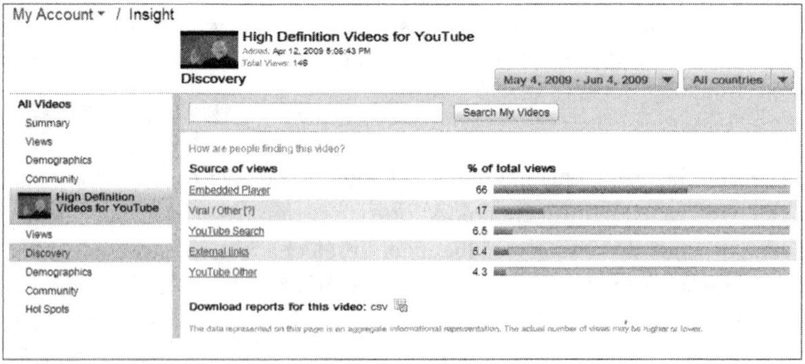

FIGURE 22.3 Using the Insight Discovery tab to determine how viewers are finding your videos.

TIP: **More Data**

Click a particular discovery method to see a list of specific items related to that method. For example, when you click the YouTube Search link, you see a list of the top search queries that "found" your video. Click a query link to see all the results for that query, and where your video appears on the results list.

Insight Demographics

When you want to learn more about who's watching your videos, click the Insight Demographics tab. This displays two charts: The first chart displays your video's viewership by age range; the second displays viewership by gender. Click a segment of either chart to view the gender makeup of an age range or to see an age range chart for a gender.

Insight Community

Click the Insight Community tab to learn more about the users who are commenting on your videos. This tab displays a timeline of when viewers have commented, as well as a map of where these users come from.

Insight Hot Spots

The Insight Hot Spots tab is a good way to compare the popularity of your video with that of other videos. It shows how "hot" your video is compared to videos of similar length.

Tracking Performance of All Your Videos

YouTube's Insight tool not only examines each of your videos individually, but also provides data about all your videos in total. To view your collective statistics, click the Account link at the top of any YouTube page; when your My Account page appears, click the Insight link for your channel.

This displays the Insight All Videos page. There are four tabs on this page: Summary, Views, Demographics, and Community. The last three tabs are similar to the same-named Insight tabs for individual videos; the Summary tab, however, is new and unique.

As you can see in Figure 22.4, the Insight All Videos Summary tab displays key information about your videos' performances at a glance. There's a graph that details total views, a chart that tells you what percentage of total views are contributed by which videos, a demographic (age and gender) chart for your channel, and a map that displays the popularity of your videos compared to those of other uploaders.

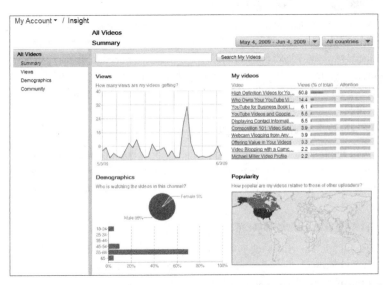

FIGURE 22.4 Viewing a performance summary for all the videos in your channel.

> TIP: **Filters**
> Use the pull-down buttons at the top of the Insight All Videos Summary tab to filter the data by date and country/region.

Summary

In this lesson, you learned how to track the viewership of your videos. In the next lesson, you learn how to manage the details of your YouTube account.

Managing Your YouTube Account

In this lesson, you learn how to edit the details of your YouTube profile and account.

Editing Your Profile

As with any online service, sometimes you need to do a bit of housekeeping with regard to the details of your YouTube profile and account. Most of these details are managed from the My Account page, which you access by clicking the Account link at the top of any YouTube page.

To edit your YouTube profile, click the Profile Setup link on the left side of the My Account page. This displays the Profile Setup page, shown in Figure 23.1. From here you can change any of the following details:

- ▶ **About Me.** A description of yourself, your website URL, and a profile picture (a frame grabbed from a selected video or an uploaded image)

- ▶ **Personal Details.** Your name, gender, age, and relationship status

- ▶ **Hometown/Location.** Where you live

- ▶ **Jobs/Career.** Your occupations and the companies you've worked for

- ▶ **Education.** Schools you've attended

- ▶ **Interests.** Your hobbies, along with your favorite movies, TV shows, music, and books

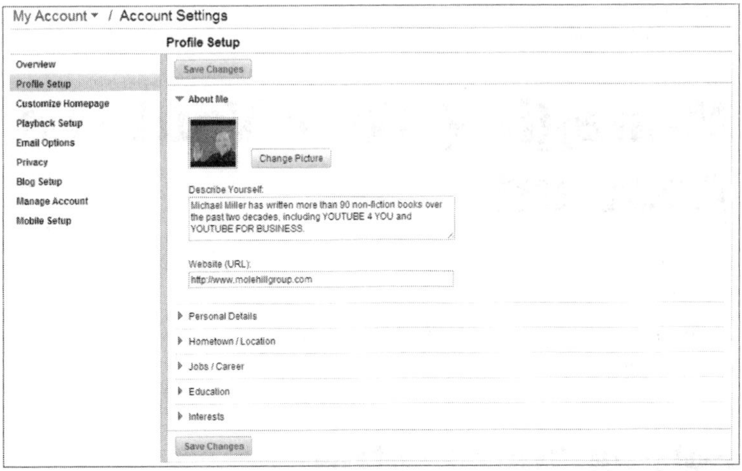

FIGURE 23.1   Editing your YouTube profile.

Click the Save Changes button to apply any changes you make.

Changing Your Email Address

What do you do if you change email addresses? Well, you'll need to change the email address you registered with YouTube. To do this, click the Email Options link on the left side of the My Account page. Enter your new email address and your current YouTube password, then click the Save Changes button.

Changing Your Password

It's good security to change your password from time to time, just in case someone is trying to hack into your YouTube account. To change your YouTube password, click the Manage Account link on the left side of the My Account page and then select the Change Password option. Enter your old password, then your new password (twice), then click the Change Password button.

Managing Privacy and Email Settings

Want better control over what other users know about you—and of what emails you receive? There are options for these settings, too.

To change your privacy settings, click the Privacy link on the left side of the My Accounts page, shown in Figure 23.2. Here you can change the following:

▶ **Search and Contact Restrictions.** Allow only your friends to send messages or share videos, or let others find your channel on YouTube only if they have your email address

▶ **Active Sharing.** When enabled, lets others see what videos you've watched; a list of recently watched videos will also appear on your channel page

▶ **Recent Activity.** Determines which actions appear in your channel page's Recent Activity box

▶ **Advertising Settings.** Uncheck if you don't want YouTube (and third-party partners) to use your personal info to target the ads they send.

FIGURE 23.2   Editing your privacy settings.

As you can see, some of these so-called privacy settings affect which email messages you receive. You can control emails even more closely by clicking the Email Options link on the left side of the My Accounts page. From here you can configure the following:

- **How Often YouTube Can Email Me.** Determines which YouTube-related events trigger email messages to you

- **Subscription and YouTube Updates.** Determines whether or not you receive weekly email updates notifying you of new subscribed videos, and also (again) whether third parties can email you with advertising

Customizing Playback

There's one final setting you might want to configure. Go to the My Account page and click the Playback Setup link on the left side of the page, shown in Figure 23.3. You can now choose a default setting for viewing videos on YouTube:

- Choose my video quality dynamically based on the current connection speed. (Default setting.)

- I have a slow connection. Never play high-quality video. (Good if you have a dial-up Internet connection.)

- I have a fast connection. Always play higher-quality video when it's available. (Triggers default playback of videos in the HQ mode.)

From this page you can also choose whether you see annotations on annotated videos. Check the Show Annotations option to display annotations overlaid on the videos; uncheck this option to view "clean" videos without annotation overlays.

My Account ▾ / Account Settings	
	Playback Setup
Overview	[Save Changes]
Profile Setup	
Customize Homepage	▼ Video Playback Quality
Playback Setup	Choose the default setting for viewing videos
Email Options	◉ Choose my video quality dynamically based on the current connection speed
Privacy	○ I have a slow connection. Never play higher-quality video.
Blog Setup	○ I have a fast connection. Always play higher-quality video when it's available.
Mobile Setup	▼ Annotations
Manage Account	Choose the default setting for displaying annotations when watching movies.
	☑ Show annotations
	[Save Changes]

FIGURE 23.3   Editing your video playback settings.

Summary

In this lesson, you learned how to configure various YouTube account settings. In the next lesson, you learn how to communicate with other YouTube users.

Communicating with Other YouTube Users

In this lesson, you learn how to contact other YouTube users and create a friends list.

Sending and Receiving YouTube Email

Commenting publically on another user's video is one thing, but sometimes you want to comment more directly—and in private. That's why YouTube has its own internal email system, which enables its users to send and receive email messages via the YouTube site.

Sending Email Messages

Sending an email message to a YouTube user is relatively easy and it's done from within your web browser. Follow these steps:

1. Click the user's name on any video or search results page to go to that user's channel page.

2. Go to the user's profile box, shown in Figure 24.1, and click Send Message.

3. When the Compose page appears, as shown in Figure 24.2, enter the subject of your message into the Subject box.

FIGURE 24.1   Click the Send Message link on the user's channel page.

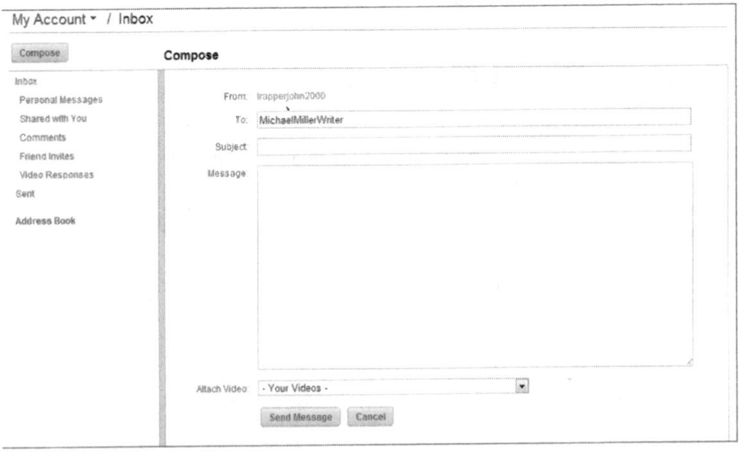

FIGURE 24.2   Sending an email message to another YouTube user.

4. Enter the text of your message into the Message box.

5. If you want to attach one of your videos to the message, pull down the Attach Video list and select the video.

6. Click the Send Message button.

Your message will now appear in that user's YouTube email inbox.

Reading Messages from Other Users

Messages that other users send to you end up in your YouTube inbox. To view and read your messages, follow these steps.

1. Click the Email icon at the top of any YouTube page.

2. When the Inbox page appears, make sure Personal Messages is selected on the left side of the page.

3. Links to all your email messages appear on this page; the subjects of your unread messages appear in bold. To read a message, click that message; this expands the message within the list, as shown in Figure 24.3.

4. To reply to the message, click the Reply button.

5. To delete the message, click the Delete button.

TIP: **Other Messages**
Your Inbox page also contains other types of messages sent via the YouTube system; these appear as links on the left side of the page. These messages include videos shared by other users (the Shared with You link), Comments from users on your videos, invitations to a friend to other users (Friend Invites), and Video Responses to your videos.

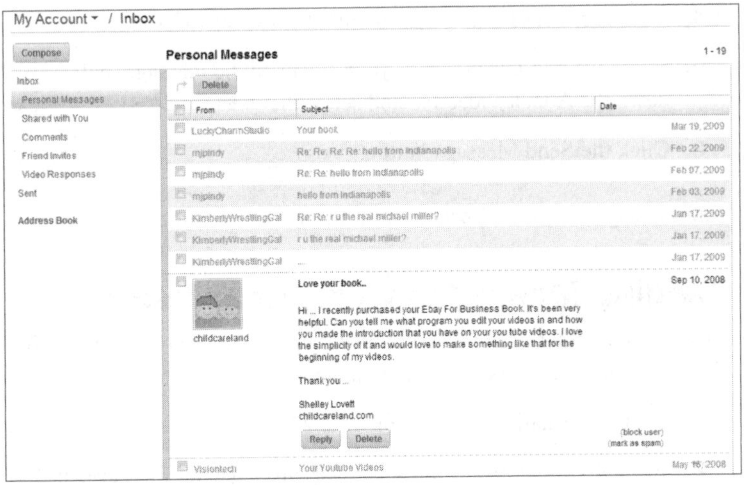

FIGURE 24.3   Viewing messages in your YouTube inbox.

Working with Friends

YouTube also lets you create lists of users with whom you can share your videos. Your YouTube friends list is kind of like the friends and buddy lists found on Facebook and in most instant-messaging programs. One click on a friend's name lets you share your videos with that person.

Adding a Friend to Your List

Adding an existing YouTube member to your friends list is relatively easy. Just follow these steps:

1. Click the user's name on any video or search results page to go to that user's channel page.

2. Go to the Connect To box and click Add as Friend.

That's it. YouTube now sends an invitation to this person to be your friend; if she accepts, she's added to your friends list.

Sending Messages to Your Friends

Your friends are automatically added to your YouTube address book, which also contains the YouTube addresses of people who subscribe to your channel and people whose channels you subscribe to. When you want to send a message to someone in your friends list, follow these steps:

1. Click the Email icon at the top of any YouTube page.

2. When the Inbox page appears, click the Address Book link on the left side of the page.

3. The Address Book page, shown in Figure 24.4, lists all your contacts—including your friends. Check the name of the person to whom you want to send a message. You can check multiple names to send a message to more than one person.

4. Click the Compose button.

5. When the Compose page appears, enter the subject of your message into the Subject box.

6. Enter the text of your message into the Message box.

7. If you want to attach one of your videos to the message, pull down the Attach Video list and select the video.

8. Click the Send Message button.

Your message is now sent to all the friends you specified.

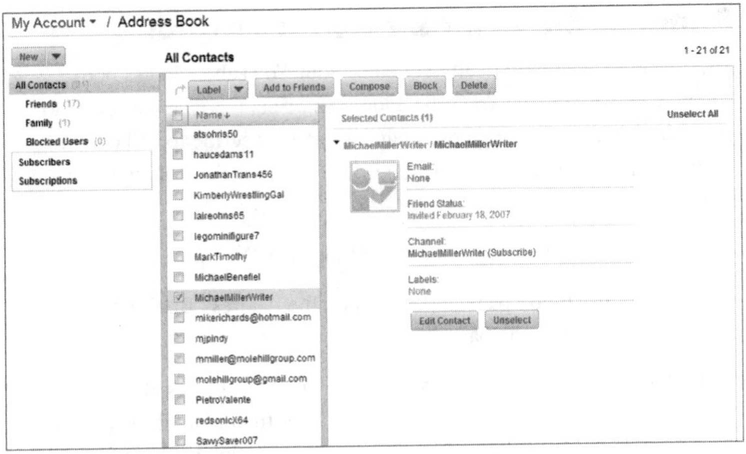

FIGURE 24.4   Viewing your YouTube address book.

Summary

In this lesson, you learned how to send messages to other YouTube users and how to add users to your friends list. In the next lesson, you learn to watch YouTube on large computer and TV displays.

LESSON 25

Watching YouTube XL on Large Displays

In this lesson, you learn how to watch YouTube on large computer and television displays.

Introducing YouTube XL

Most people watch YouTube on their computer monitors. Because most monitors run from 15" to 19" diagonally, that's a pretty small picture—not nearly as large as what you have on your living room TV.

But some users have larger monitors, which makes watching YouTube videos more like watching movies on TV. And there's always the option of connecting your computer to your TV, which allows you to watch all your favorite YouTube videos on the bigger screen.

The problem with using the normal YouTube site for big-screen viewing is that…well, everything on it is designed for viewing close-up on a computer monitor. It's what we call the 10-inch interface, something you can literally reach out and touch. When you're viewing on a larger computer or television display, you're sitting further from the screen; so you need a 10-*foot* interface instead.

To that end, YouTube has introduced a sub-site that provides that type of 10-foot interface for big-screen viewers. The new site is called YouTube XL, and it's located at www.youtube.com/xl.

Viewing YouTube XL

As you can see in Figure 25.1, YouTube XL doesn't look at all like the main YouTube site. Everything here is nice and big, big enough to view comfortable at a 10-foot distance.

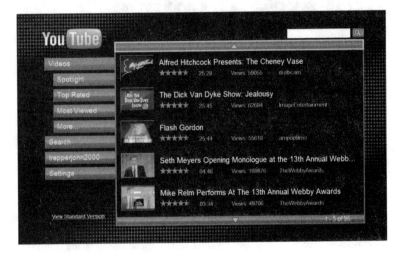

FIGURE 25.1   The YouTube XL main page—for extra-large displays.

Navigating the Main Page

You navigate the YouTube XL site by using the navigation tabs at the left side of the page. There are four main tabs: Videos, Search, *Username*, and Settings. When you click the Videos or *Username* tab you see additional tabs. In all, here are the available tabs on the main YouTube XL page:

▶ **Spotlight.** Under the main Videos tab, YouTube's recommended videos of the day

▶ **Top Rated.** Under the main Videos tab, those videos that have received the highest viewer ratings

▶ **Most Viewed.** Under the main Videos tab, the most-viewed videos today

▶ **More.** Click this tab (under the main Videos tab) to view videos in the following categories: Recently Added, Most Popular, Most Discussed, Rising Videos, Top Favorited, Most Responded, Top Music, Top Major Label Music, Top Indie Music, Top Unsigned Music, Education

▶ **Search.** Clicking this tab displays a Search for Videos box

▶ **My Videos.** Under the *Username* tab, displays the videos you've uploaded

▶ **Favorites.** Under the *Username* tab, displays the videos in your Favorites list

▶ **Playlists.** Under the *Username* tab, displays your collected playlists

▶ **Sign Out.** Click this tab (under the *Username* tab) to sign out of the YouTube site

▶ **Settings.** Displays two primary settings: Play Next Video When Current Video Ends and Filter Videos That May Not Be Suitable for Minors. Also lets you configure language and geography settings for your account

Searching YouTube XL

You find videos on YouTube XL either by browsing the main categories under the Videos tab or by searching. You can search either from the Search box at the top-right corner of the main page or by clicking the Search tab (shown in Figure 25.2). With each approach, use your computer keyboard to enter your search query into the Search box, then click the Search button. Your search results are displayed on the next page.

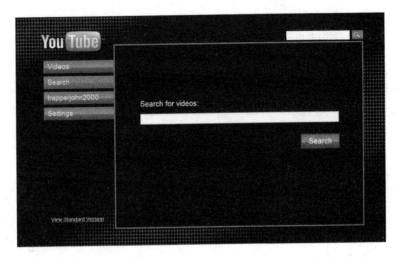

FIGURE 25.2   Searching YouTube XL.

Playing XL Videos

Whether you're browsing through the categories or viewing search results, YouTube XL displays five videos per screen. You scroll through the video list by clicking the up or down arrows above and below the list; this displays another five videos.

To view a video, simply click its thumbnail. This displays the large video viewing window shown in Figure 25.3. As with the regular YouTube site, XL videos begin playback automatically.

Playback controls are overlaid on the video when you hover your cursor over the video playback window. These are simplified (and enlarged) versions of normal YouTube playback controls—Play/Pause, Previous (video), Next (video), Shuffle, and Fullscreen.

Below the video playback window are five buttons:

▶ **Favorite.** Click this button to add this video to your Favorites list.

▶ **Flag.** Click this button to flag a video that contains inappropriate or infringing content.

FIGURE 25.3   Viewing a YouTube XL video.

▶ **Share.** Click this button to send an email about this video to others. When you click the Share button, the panel to the right of
the video changes to display an Email box (enter the recipient's
address) and Message box; click the Send button to send the
email message, containing a link to the video.

▶ **Info.** Click to display information about the video—the user's
name, when the video was added, number of views, and the star
rating.

▶ **Related.** Click to display videos related to this video.

Click each button to activate its function.

To return to the YouTube XL main page, click the large left arrow to the
left of the video player window.

Playing XL Videos Full Screen

If you're viewing YouTube XL on a large display, you probably want to
take full advantage of that big screen—which means ditching everything
around the video player and viewing the video itself full screen. This is an

especially good idea if you're watching an HD video on an HDTV display.

To view a YouTube XL video full screen, simply click the Full Screen button at the lower-right corner of the video player display. To return to regular viewing mode, press the Esc button on your computer keyboard.

Connecting Your Computer to Your TV Display

There's one last item to discuss in regard to watching YouTube XL on large displays. Just how do you connect your computer to your television set?

The answer to this question depends on what types of connectors you have on both your computer and your television set. In general, you need to do a same-to-same connection; that is, connect a cable from a particular type of output jack on your computer to that same type of input jack on your TV. Most newer TVs have a full complement of input jacks, which makes this task easier; if you have an older TV, your options might be limited—or not exist at all.

Depending on your computer, you might find some or all of the following video connectors, all shown in Figure 25.4:

- ▶ **VGA.** This is a small trapezoidal connector found on almost all computers, used to connect computers to computer monitors. Few TVs have VGA connectors, so this probably isn't the best way to go. (If you go this route, you'll have to run separate right and left audio cables—sometimes attached to a "Y" connector—from your computer's audio output or headphone jacks to your TV; VGA transmits only video signals.)

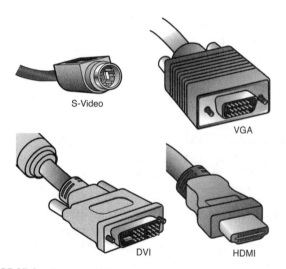

FIGURE 25.4   Common video connectors.

▶ **DVI.** Many newer computers have this type of digital video connection. This is another input that most TVs don't have. However, converting DVI to HDMI is fairly easy. All you need is a DVI-to-HDMI converter cable or adapter, which you can find at your local electronics store. You can then connect the DVI output from your computer to the HDMI input found on most newer TVs. (Since DVI only transmits video signals, you'll have to run separate right and left audio cables from your computer to your TV.)

▶ **HDMI**. If you're fortunate enough to have an HDMI output on your computer, use an HDMI cable to connect it directly to the HDMI input on your TV. HDMI transmits the best signal from computer to TV. (HDMI transmits both video and audio signals, so no separate audio cable is necessary.)

► **S-Video**. Some computers have a simple S-Video connector. This is an older type of connector and passes a lower-resolution video signal. It's usable, but not ideal. (Since S-Video transmits only video signals, you'll have to run separate right and left audio cables from your computer to your TV.)

CAUTION: **Low Resolution**

S-Video is only good for standard definition or YouTube HQ videos. It cannot pass the high definition signal found in YouTube HD videos.

What do you do if your computer only has a VGA video output? You're not completely out of luck. Several companies sell affordable VGA to S-Video converter boxes, as well as more expensive VGA to HDMI converter boxes. Check with your local electronics store for more details.

TIP: **Wireless Keyboard**

Even if you get your computer connected to your TV, you still have to use your mouse and keyboard to navigate the YouTube XL site. You might want to invest in a wireless keyboard and mouse that you can use from across the room.

Summary

In this lesson, you learned how to watch videos on the big screen with YouTube XL. In the next and final lesson, you learn how to promote the videos you upload to the YouTube site.

Promoting Your YouTube Videos

In this lesson, you learn how to attract viewers to the videos you upload.

Getting the Content Right

With millions and millions of videos on the YouTube site, how do you attract viewers to the videos you upload? It all starts with having a video that people want to watch—and that they'll share with their friends.

The most popular YouTube videos offer something valuable to viewers. In general, people watch videos that do one of three things: entertain, inform, or educate. If your video performs one of these functions, you stand a much better chance of attracting large numbers of viewers.

Entertaining Videos

Most videos on YouTube strive to be entertaining. Whether it's cute kittens, stupid human tricks, or wryly humorous video blog postings, the typical YouTube video attracts via some measure of entertainment value.

What makes a video entertaining? Unfortunately, when it comes to entertainment, there are no rules. Some videos entertain by being funny, others by being heartwarming, others by being inspiring. What matters is creativity—creating something that viewers want to watch over and over again.

Informative Videos

Another thing that attracts viewers is information—in particular, information that is specifically relevant and useful. We're talking about the latest news here, tailor-made for the target YouTube customer.

Do you have news about a topic with broad interest? Then share that news with the YouTube community, either via a short video "newscast" or in a video blog. This type of video doesn't have to be fancy; a simple talking head is all it takes to convey important information. Just make sure it's timely (last month's news isn't new anymore), accurate, and of interest to a large number of viewers.

TIP: **Authority**
If you can establish yourself as an authority on a given subject, you can gain repeat viewers who subscribe to your informative videos.

Educational Videos

In a similar fashion, anytime you can help someone learn how to do something that they need to do, you'll attract eyeballs. Show mechanically inept viewers how to the change the oil in their cars, or teach would-be chefs how to prepare a gourmet meal, and you'll gain praise for the help you provide. Step-by-step instruction attracts large numbers of viewers in today's increasingly do-it-yourself world—as witnessed by the success of HGTV and the Food Network on cable television.

The key to creating an educational video is to work through the instructions, step-by-step. Storyboard the video in advance so you can shoot all the shots at multiple camera angles, and then piece together the shots using a video-editing program. Instructional videos can be a little longer than the two to three minutes I typically recommend, especially if the subject at hand takes longer to explain. Take the time you need (up to YouTube's 10-minute limit) and go into as much detail as necessary. The more expert help you provide, the more viewers you'll attract.

PLAIN ENGLISH: **Storyboard**
A series of rough sketches that outline the scenes in a video.

Optimize Your Video for Search

How do users find videos on YouTube? Many people email links of their favorite videos to friends, of course, which is how videos go viral. But most viewers find the videos they want the same way they find anything on the Internet—by searching for them.

This means that you need to optimize your videos for search. The higher your videos appear in the search results, the more viewers you'll get. (That's because most users don't scroll through pages and pages of search results; you want to be as high up as possible on the first page of search results to capture the most click-throughs.)

Choose the Right Tags

When it comes to making viewers aware of your videos, remember the tags—those keywords that viewers use to search for videos on YouTube. Without the right tags, great content will go unfound; add the appropriate tags, and you make it easier for viewers to find your videos.

> NOTE: **Tags**
> A YouTube tag is the same thing as a keyword on a website.

To optimize the tags you apply to your video, you have to think like the viewer. Get inside the heads of your potential viewers and think how they might search for the information they need. When you figure out the key-words they'll most likely search for, you have the most effective tags for your video.

Your tags should include a combination of both generic and specific key-words. For example, if your video talks about the differences between incandescent and fluorescent lighting, you should include generic tags such as *lighting, light bulb, energy efficient*, and the like, as well as more specific tags such as *incandescent* and *fluorescent*. This way you'll attract viewers who are essentially browsing or just getting interested in the topic, while also making yourself known to those viewers who have more specific needs in mind—or who are better versed in the technical lingo.

Write a Compelling Title

The title of your video is another key to attracting viewers. Not only is your title searched by YouTube when users submit queries, it's also how most viewers determine what your video is about.

Yes, the full description is there to read, but most people skim rather than read—especially when they're browsing through a page full of search results. So your title has to not only include the most important keywords or tags, but also convey the content of the video.

That means, of course, that you have to create a concise, descriptive, and compelling title. It's copywriting at its finest, distilling the essence of what you have to offer in a very short line of copy. It takes a lot of work and experience to get right.

Pick the Best Thumbnail Image

Finally, remember what a typical YouTube search results page looks like—lots of video listings, each accompanied by a single thumbnail image. You need to attract viewers to your specific listing in the search results—which means presenting the most attractive and relevant thumbnail image possible.

As you learned in Lesson 16, "Editing Video Information," YouTube lets you choose from three possible images to use as your video's thumbnail image. You need to pick the thumbnail that looks best on the search results page—and the one that best represents what your video is about.

The best thumbnails are clear, not blurry, and have a dominant subject— ideally a person's face or a close-up of an important or interesting item. You might also stand out from the other listings with a brightly colored or high contrast image in your thumbnail—anything to make the thumbnail "pop" on the search results page.

Sharing with Friends and Contacts

Beyond optimizing your videos for search, you can use the YouTube community itself to promote your videos. One of the most effective forms of promotion is to let your friends and subscribers know about the new videos you upload.

Promoting your video to subscribers is easy—YouTube does the work for you. Whenever you post a new video to the YouTube site, YouTube automatically sends an email to all of your channel's subscribers informing them of the video. That's easy.

More work is necessary to notify your friends of your latest video. Go to the page for that video and click the Share link under the video player. To send a message to all your friends, click the Add All Friends link in the scrolling list; to send a message to all your contacts, click the Add All Contacts link. Then enter your message (something along the lines of "Check out my latest video") to the Message box and click the Send button.

Advertising Your Videos

There's another way to promote your videos to other YouTube viewers, although it's not free. YouTube now offers pay-per-click keyword advertising for any video you have uploaded on the YouTube site.

PLAIN ENGLISH: **Pay Per Click (PPC)**
A form of online advertising where the advertiser pays for each user that clicks on the ad.

YouTube calls these ads "promoted videos," and they're found on the right side of most search results pages, as shown in Figure 26.1. Each ad includes a brief text description and link, as well as a video thumbnail. When a user clicks on the ad or thumbnail, they're taken to your video page—and you're charged for it.

FIGURE 26.1   Promoted videos on a YouTube search results page.

Understanding Promoted Videos

That's the way pay-per-click advertising works. You don't pay to place the ad; you're charged only when someone clicks on it. You pay a certain price per click (PPC), typically a few pennies. The more clicks you get, the more you pay—and, presumably, the more viewers you accrue.

To get started, you select a keyword or group of keywords that best describe your video. You "purchase" these keywords and select how much you're willing to pay for each click. When someone searches for a keyword that you've purchased, your ad will appear on that person's search results page, in the Promoted Videos section. At that point your account is charged for the click, at the previously agreed-upon rate.

Of course, you also set a total budget for your campaign. When your PPC charges reach this amount, your ad is disabled. You determine how much you're willing to spend each month, and your advertising charges will never exceed this amount.

NOTE: **Google AdWords**

YouTube's Promoted Videos program is part of Google's AdWords PPC advertising service. To advertise using Promoted Videos, you must have a Google AdWords account. Learn more at adwords.google.com.

Signing Up for Promoted Videos

To advertise a specific video on the YouTube site, follow these steps:

1. Click your username at the top of any YouTube page, then select My Videos.

2. When the My Videos page appears, click the Promote button for the video you want to promote.

> NOTE: **Individual Promotions**
>
> You promote each video individually. You can set up separate campaigns for different videos, but you can't set up a generic campaign for all your videos.

3. This takes you to a page that describes YouTube's Promoted Videos program. To proceed, click the Add Promoted Videos to My YouTube Account Now! link.

4. If you're not yet a member of Google's AdWords program, you'll be prompted to sign up and enter your payment information. If you're already an AdWords advertiser, you'll go directly to the Set Budget page.

5. When the Set Budget page appears, enter the total amount of money you're willing to spend per day, then click the OK, I Want to Use This Budget button.

6. When the Summary page appears, click the Create a New Promotion link.

7. When the Choose Video page appears, click the video you want to promote, and then click the Next, I Agree button.

8. When the Write Your Promotion page appears, as shown in Figure 26.2, enter a title in the first box, followed by two lines of text for your ad. The title must be 25 words or less; each line of text must be 35 words or less.

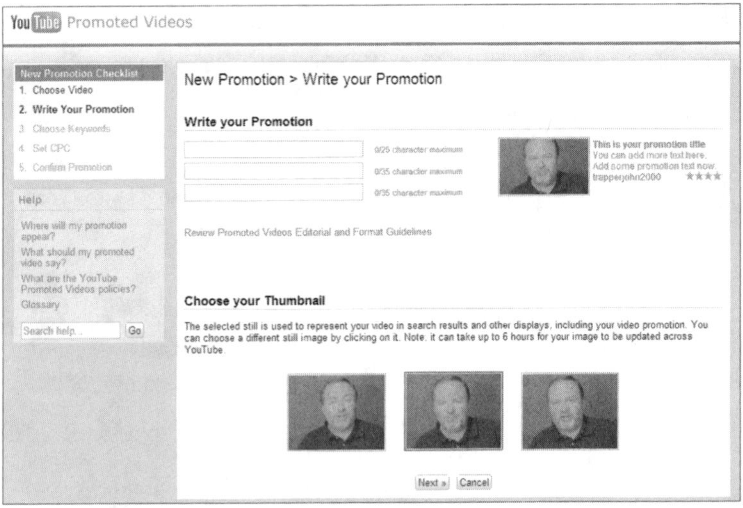

FIGURE 26.2   Creating the ad for a promoted video.

9. Select the thumbnail to use for the ad, then click Next.

10. You now see the Choose Keywords page. Enter a group of keywords or phrases that best describes your video, with each keyword or phrase on a separate line, and then click the Next button.

11. When the Set CPC page appears, enter the amount you're willing to pay per click, then click the Next button.

12. When the Review Your Promotion page appears, click the Okay, Run My Promotion! button.

PLAIN ENGLISH: **Cost Per Click (CPC)**
The amount you're willing to pay for each click on your ad.

> TIP: **Set Your Price**
>
> The higher the CPC you set, the more likely your ad will place high on matching search results pages. That's because YouTube assigns placement based on bids by multiple advertisers. Set too low a CPC, and higher-bidding advertisers for a given keyword will have their ads appear higher and more often.

Your ad is now added to YouTube's promoted videos database. It will appear on search results pages when someone searches for one of the keywords you entered.

Tracking Performance

You track the performance of your promoted videos—and manage your campaigns—with the Promoted Videos Dashboard. You access this page by going to ads.youtube.com/dashboard.

The Dashboard Summary page, shown in Figure 26.3, displays key information about your current campaigns. This information includes the number of impressions (page views) and clicks for each ad, as well as the click through rate (CTR), average cost per click, and total cost of the campaign. You can also use this page to pause, resume, and delete individual campaigns, as well as create new promotions.

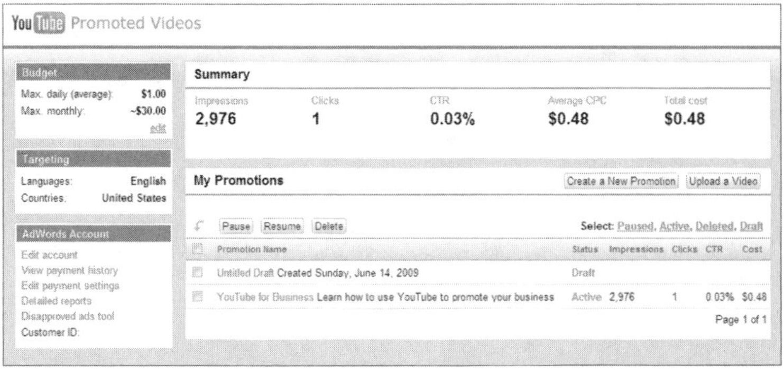

FIGURE 26.3 Tracking results with the Dashboard Summary.

> PLAIN ENGLISH: **Click Through Rate (CTR)**
>
> The number of times an ad is clicked versus the number of times the page it appears on is viewed, expressed as a percentage.

Promoting Outside of YouTube

Finally, don't forget that you can promote your YouTube videos outside of the YouTube site. All forms of online and traditional marketing can be used to promote your videos, including email marketing, blog marketing, social network marketing, banner ads, and the like. Just include a link to an individual video or your YouTube channel in your marketing materials, so everyone can see for themselves what you're talking about.

Summary

In this final lesson, you learned how to promote the videos you upload to the YouTube site. I wish you success in attracting lots of viewers!

Index

O

offensive videos, reporting, 28-29

optimizing videos for search
> tags, 173
> thumbnail images, 174
> titles, 174

P

partner videos, downloading, 65

passwords, changing, 152

pausing video playback, 25

pay-per-click (PPC) advertising, 175

PCs, connecting to TV display, 168, 170

People & Blog category, 15

personalizing channel pages, 140-141
> channel modules, 143
> channel settings, 142
> themes and colors, 142

Pets & Animals category, 15

pixels, 31

Play All button, 45

playback, customizing, 154

Playback Setup link, 154

playing videos
> annotated videos, 131, 154
> closed captioned videos, 126
> connecting computer to TV display, 168-170
> customizing playback, 154
> downloaded videos, 67-68

in full-screen mode, 25, 32

HD (high-definition) videos, 33-34

HQ (high-quality) videos, 33

on iPhone, 77-78

resolution, 31-32

with video player, 24-26

YouTube XL videos, 166-168

playlists
> adding favorites to, 38-39, 44
> adding videos to, 43
> creating, 41-42
> definition of, 41
> deleting, 46
> editing, 45-46
> sharing, 46, 53-54
> viewing, 44-45

Playlists tab (YouTube XL), 165

popularity of YouTube, 3

positioning subjects, 90-91

posting videos to blogs, 63-64

PPC (pay-per-click) advertising, 175

Privacy link, 153

privacy settings, 153-154

Profile Setup page, 151

profiles, editing, 151-152

programs
> closed caption software programs, 124
> video-editing programs, 95-97

editing videos with, 97-98

Promote button, 177

X-Y-Z

SamsTeachYourself

from Sams Publishing

Sams Teach Yourself in 10 Minutes
offers straightforward, practical answers
for fast results.

These small books of 250 pages or less
offer tips that point out shortcuts and
solutions, cautions that help you avoid
common pitfalls, notes that explain
additional concepts, and provide additional
information. By working through the
10-minute lessons, you learn everything
you need to know quickly and easily!

When you only have time for the answers,
Sams Teach Yourself books are your
best solution.

Visit **informit.com/samsteachyourself**
for a complete listing of the products
available.

FREE Online Edition

Your purchase of **Sams Teach Yourself YouTube in 10 Minutes** includes access to a free online edition for 45 days through the Safari Books Online subscription service. Nearly every Sams book is available online through Safari Books Online, along with more than 5,000 other technical books and videos from publishers such as Addison-Wesley Professional, Cisco Press, Exam Cram, IBM Press, O'Reilly, Prentice Hall, and Que.

SAFARI BOOKS ONLINE allows you to search for a specific answer, cut and paste code, download chapters, and stay current with emerging technologies.

Activate your FREE Online Edition at www.informit.com/safarifree

STEP 1: Enter the coupon code: JBHXZAA.

STEP 2: New Safari users, complete the brief registration form. Safari subscribers, just log in.

If you have difficulty registering on Safari or accessing the online edition, please e-mail customer-service@safaribooksonline.com